THE SOCIAL DEMOCRATS

The Social Democrats

Those Who Went and Those Who Stayed

Ken Coates

The Forward March of Labour Halted?

Spokesman

First published in 1983 by:
Spokesman
Bertrand Russell House
Gamble Street
Nottingham

British Library Cataloguing in Publication Data:
Coates, Ken
The social democrats.
1. Socialism — Great Britain
I. Title
335.5'0941   HX244
ISBN 0 85124 357 6
ISBN 0 85124 358 4 Pbk

Printed by the Russell Press Ltd., Nottingham

Contents

Acknowledgements

Earlier versions of some of the pieces in this book appeared in *What Went Wrong* (Spokesman/IWC, 1979), *How to Win?* (Spokesman/IWC, 1981), *New Left Review* (No.135), *Labour Weekly*, *Tribune* and *Thesis Eleven*. Grateful acknowledgement is made to these publications.

Foreword

The papers which make up this little book were prepared between the Labour defeat of 1979, and the debacle of 1983. There was, as the press never tires of reminding us, a period of stern recrimination inside the Labour Party throughout that period. Outside it, breakaway forces added their own contribution to the general clamour.

Increasingly it becomes apparent that the crisis in the Labour Party reflects a deeper crisis in the state of Britain, as most of the more potent industrial and economic influences adjust to international forms of organisation, whilst at the same time doing what they can to disconnect the residual traditions of national democracy from any surviving effective mechanisms of power. Even when the Labour Party wins an election, we find the International Monetary Fund deciding how much scope it shall have for action. Military alliances impose affinities which bear no relation to national needs and stoke up enmities which are not our own.

After the doleful experience of the first Wilson Government, I published a collection of writings under the title *The Crisis of British Socialism*. Today's crisis would more properly be styled a crisis of European socialism, since the slump locks most European states into the same dismal patterns of monetarism and militarism and brings all nearer to a day when action for recovery by their democratic forces will have to be undertaken jointly or not at all. At present there remains, of course, a diminishing scope for purely national action. In Britain this is conditioned by the flow of North Sea oil. This will prove finite. But until we can find the means to assert our common priorities on an appropriately international scale, defending our peoples against the exploitative internationals of capital and cold war, we are, each of us, all too likely to continue to lose ground nationally even while our national democratic heritages are continuously undermined.

It may seem a defiant act to publish these contributions to a debate which is widely regarded as having been unedifying. Nonetheless, if what was said here was true, it bears repetition. As the Labour movement prepares to occupy new ground, it is only reasonable to leave the old territory as tidy as possible.

CHAPTER ONE

The Fall of the
Callaghan Administration

The decade from 1970 to 1979 entered, and left, to the sound of Labour Governments falling: a noise which sometimes includes a certain amount of recrimination, but which never fails to offer a positively deafening volume of apologetics.

In 1970, the recrimination came from Mr Prentice, who felt that the deceased administration had not been quite socialist enough.[1] The justifications came from Mr Wilson himself, who no sooner picked himself up from the steps of Downing Street than he set about compiling 993 pages of vigorous, and by no means entirely self-effacing, instant history. He concluded this work with these words:

> "No incoming Prime Minister, if Mr Heath takes over, in living memory has taken over a stronger economic situation. I wanted to use that as we have never been able to, in the past five or six years, to use the economic situation for building on what we have done, for example in the social services, health and education and social security and housing — to accelerate what we have been doing, to intensify and develop it. Now we hand over the means to do that, to somebody else."[2]

If, in 1979, Mr Callaghan could not offer similar comfort, this is not only because he is somewhat more modest than his predecessor. The truth is, Mr Callaghan had presided over what had been fundamentally, as well as in name, a liberal-labour coalition, covering for the International Monetary Fund. He had struggled to ride out a prolonged slump, in the hope of securing re-election during the few moments whilst the world economy rose over a minor bump of upturn before plummeting again down the next precipitous switchback. Within the restricted scope afforded by its creditors, his administration had tried to act humanely, by generating artificial youth employment measures, distributing small amounts of money for inner-city rehabilitation, and a host of similar palliatives. But within the hostile world setting, the de-industrialisation of Britain continued its gathering decline, British competivity in manufacturing markets showed none of the prayed-for signs of recovery, import domination of key sectors of home trade continued. This manifest rot was not stopped by the oil boom if its effects were temporarily offset.

The result of this baleful evolution has been a different style of apologia. It sometimes seems as if, the more harmful and stupid the measures actually taken, the more fertile the explanatory imagination. This is only true *sometimes*, however. Other times are so dismal that even the muse of plausible double-talk, so dependable a standby on most front benches, takes fear and flies. Here, for instance, is the anonymous judgement of *Labour Victory*, the organ of the Campaign for Labour Victory, a notable group of defenders of official inaction on almost every possible front. It begins well:

> "In 1979, we faced the electorate with a leadership that was outstanding, a record of achievement that was considerable and a promise for the future we honestly felt we could perform."

But in the next breath we are told

> "there was no way the Government could avoid a big rise in unemployment and a sharp fall in living standards, at least temporarily."

Immediately afterwards, in defence of the IMF, we learn

> "the IMF crisis became inevitable because we were too slow to adjust our spending plans, which had risen by 10% in two years, when there was no growth in the national economy at all."[3]

But who was responsible for this slow adjustment? Why, who else but the same "outstanding" leadership which subsequently so obediently "adjusted its spending plans" when invited by the IMF? And did not the "considerable" achievement include "a big rise in unemployment" and all the rest of it? As for the "promise for the future", what was it but more of the same, guaranteed to generate a need for still more of the same?

The apostasy involved in this "temporary" adjustment was not something restricted to the betrayal of the ideals of Michael Foot, or the sacred memory of Aneurin Bevan, or any of the other hallowed idols of the left. It struck right at the heart of the announced doctrines of the self-styled 'revisionist' thinkers, whichever version of the complex of ideas associated with this grouping one might choose to take. Socialist Union, for instance, in what for the New Right was at one time the key text, *Twentieth Century Socialism*,[4] widely diffused by Penguin Books in 1956, had this to say:

"Planning for economic security means, first and foremost, planning to maintain full employment.[5] Socialists can admit no compromise with this aim, no scaling it down to 'a high and stable level of employment', no playing with the idea that 'a small dose of unemployment' might be good for production. Just as the certainty of a job is the first condition of decent living, so is full employment the first condition of a socialist economy. Even if it could be proved conclusively — and all the evidence points in the opposite direction — that a revival of the fear of unemployment would increase productivity, this would be a poor bargain and a disgraceful exchange."

If this represented the 'ethical' revisionism of Allan Flanders, there was also the 'sociological' current of C.A.R. Crosland: the main statement of which went to press in the same month as did Flanders' little book, and which spells out the precise social meaning of full employment in the dry tones of an accomplished pedagogue:

"there has been a decisive movement of power within industry itself from management to labour. This is mainly a consequence of the seller's market for labour created by full employment.

The relative strength of workers and employers does not, of course, depend solely on conditions in the labour market. It depends also on the political balance, the social climate, the degree of organisation of the two sides, and current views about the relation between wages on the one hand, and profits, employment, or the foreign balance on the other. These factors had all changed in a manner favourable to labour even before 1939. Yet the strength of the Unions was still severely limited by large-scale unemployment; and they were obviously, and knew it, the weaker of the two contenders.

The change from a buyer's to a seller's market for labour, however, by transposing at once the interests, and therefore the attitudes, of the two sides, has dramatically altered the balance of power at every level of labour relations.

At the level of the individual worker, the decisive change relates to the question of dismissal. The employee, for whom dismissal before the war was often a sentence of long-term unemployment, can now quickly find a job elsewhere; and he has lost, in consequence, his fear of the sack, and with it his docility. The employer, on the other hand, who before the war could replace a dismissed worker from a long waiting-list of applicants for jobs, may now have difficulty in finding any replacement at all; and he has acquired, in consequence, a reluctance to dismiss, and himself has become more docile. Thus the balance of advantage is reversed, and the result is a transformation of relationships at the shop-floor level.

At the level of the plant or firm, the main change lies in the altered attitude of the two sides towards their ultimate weapons of coercion — the strike and the lock-out. With unemployment, the employer can often well afford to endure a strike or initiate a lockout; the odds in the contest are on his side, while the cost of a stoppage, with stocks often high and market conditions unprofitable, may be relatively minor. But with full employment, the odds are quite different, since the workers can now hold out much longer, while the cost of a stoppage in terms of profits foregone is likely, with stocks perhaps low and a lucrative market demand, to be much greater. The employers' incentive to avoid strikes has thus increased in the same measure as the workers' prospects of winning them; the implications for the balance of power are obvious.[6]

Now, it seems reasonable to assume that if full employment (which does *not*, we agree with Socialist Union, mean simply "a high and stable level of employment") signifies, as Crosland teaches, a shift of power to workpeople, both at the level of their individual engagements and contracts, and at the level of their collective capacity to control working conditions and to bargain jointly: then mass unemployment implies a contrary shift of power, away from the workpeople. In short, the decision to allow this "disgraceful exchange", as Labour's leading social-democratic spokesmen once rightly characterised it, involved a simultaneous abandonment of the basic assumptions of Labour's revisionists, a powerful setback to workers and their organisations, and a direct breach of Labour's own Election Manifestos which had promised "a fundamental shift in the balance of wealth and power" in a direction exactly contrary to that which was in fact brought about.

Of course, as Hugh Gaitskell wrote even before he took over the Labour Party leadership,

"Our attitude to the problems of full employment has been greatly influenced by the 'Keynesian Revolution'. Indeed, one might almost say that just as the early Fabians were influenced by the Ricardian theory of rent and its development by John Stuart Mill, so their successors today have been influenced by *The General Theory of Employment . . .*"[7]

There are various things to be said about the ill-treatment meted out to Keynes by some of Gaitskell's disciples. At this point, however, we might refer to that *General Theory*, to refresh our memories about one of Keynes' more important historical insights.

"The ideas of economists and political philosophers" he wrote, in his concluding notes to that book, "both when they are right and when they are wrong, are more powerful than is commonly understood. Indeed the world is ruled by little else. Practical men, who believe themselves to be quite exempt from any intellectual influences, are usually the slaves of some defunct economist. Madmen in authority, who hear voices in the air, are distilling their frenzy from some academic scribbler of a few years back."[8]

This is a salutary thought to commend to those who have been busy for two and a half decades emancipating socialism from the domination of ideas. "The British socialist movement has not been doctrinaire in its philosophy" they have often written: "like the labour movement of which it formed a part, it was empirical and tolerant".[9] R.H. Tawney, who was taken up and patronised by this school of anti-ideologues, and who as a result of the villainies done in his name is now revolving in his grave at the speed of sound at least, once expressed his distaste for philosophies of history, to which, he told us, he maintained an attitude like that of a little London girl, who, when asked by her teacher to explain the use of pins, replied

"Pins are very useful things; they have saved many people's lives by not a-swallerin' of them."[10]

This was good advice by a historian to historians. It was, however, dangerous advice to a group of politicians, even Labour ones, more particularly when some of them might climb into or sit close by the seats of power. For such men and women, Keynes' admonishments are sounder: they are otherwise all too prone to reject general ideas for the allegedly practical option, and to throw even the most elementary sense of duty or justice into the same convenient basket in which Tawney kept the philosophy of history. The Callaghan administration was not mad, nor deliberately wicked, and if it did hear voices in the air telling it to consecrate the five-percent norm in a cathedral at Rheims, unlike St. Joan it readily recanted when it observed certain instruments being warmed on pyres outside Congress House. But it was composed of people who, in the main, had no time for doctrine, and who found themselves the more surprised to hear their own voices inadvertently talking in dilute versions of monetarist jargon, while the dole queues snaked up to a million-and-a-half in length.

It is difficult to see the results as anything other than disastrous for the Labour movement, since they have done much to legitimate the greatly worse unemployment which now pursues the electoral defeat of Mr Callaghan's team. Had the followers of Crosland and the disciples of Socialist Union held up their own banners, demanding "first and foremost" the commitment to full employment, ex social democracy would not have shrivelled to its present deformed state, which rejects 'scientific' socialism as unscientific, 'utopian' socialism as chiliastic, and its own most cherished analyses as impracticable. Such an input of scepticism would have been commendable if it could leave us with any pointer whatever to useful future action: but instead it left us only with the hardly ardent hope that if this group of tolerant and genial cynics could hang on to office, worse fates might possibly be kept at bay.

Like all such evolutions, this reduction of alleged social democracy to its opposite offers a variety of unedifying spectacles. See, there goes Mr Healey, pregnant with the whitewash bucket underneath that dirty mac, up the ladder by the barn-wall to touch up the slogans. "Four legs good, two legs better" we now read, where once it said something about squeezing until the pips squeaked.

All animals are equal, but some are more unemployed than others. If the pigs celebrated this discovery, made in the course of piecemeal social engineering, by buying a wireless, putting in the 'phone, and taking out subscriptions to *John Bull*, *Tit-bits* and the *Daily Mirror*, the ex social democrats recognised it by refusing to carry into their manifesto the Labour Party's virtually unanimous decision to abolish the House of Lords, and dressing up Hugh Scanlon in its regalia, rescued from Farmer Jones' old wardrobe. We should remember this when we listen to the speeches of moderate men about the present predicament in which our outstanding leaders have landed us. As the *Observer* put it:

"there can be no escaping the chasm that divides Left and Right. Between the Left's advocacy of import controls, greater public expenditure, and open hostility to the Common Market, and the Right's adherence to the mixed economy, lower direct taxation and free trade, the divide is deep.

David Marquand, Labour MP for Ashfield from 1967-77, gives this profoundly gloomy, but not easily disputed, analysis of the party's split condition in the current issue of *Encounter.* 'The gulf between socialists and social democrats is now the deepest in British politics . . .

'To pretend in this situation that socialists and social democrats are all part of the same great Movement — that Shirley Williams and Bill Rodgers and Roy Hattersley really have more in common with Tony Benn and Eric Heffer and Stanley Orme than they do with Peter Walker or Ian Gilmour or Edward Heath — is to live a lie. But it is a lie which the Labour Party has to live if it is to live at all'."[11]

David Marquand is an impeccable social democrat of the new

school, which "adheres to the mixed economy, lower direct taxation, and free trade": but where does he stand in relation to 'the union of ethics and politics' which Socialist Union propounded, on the material foundation of full employment? The argument in the beginning was that various items of socialist ideological baggage could now be dispensed with, since full employment had in fact brought about an "irreversible shift" in the balance of power. Having presided over the reversal of this irreversible event, the modern social democrats do not send forth messengers to retrieve that which was necessary in the intellectual legacy which they left behind. Instead, they denounce as socialists, marxists or worse all those who still hanker for some part of the old consensus upon which, once, all were adamantly agreed.

It is this parting of the ways which has brought the Labour Party to the point of splitting.

Footnotes

1. Mr Prentice's article in *Political Quarterly* (Vol.41, No.2, April-June 1970) was entitled 'Not Socialist Enough': and condemned the 'drift to the right' of a Labour Government whose members "are constantly in contact with the 'establishment'." With some prescience Mr Prentice drew up an indictment "of policies which never ought to have been followed by a Labour Government":

    "The pursuit of orthodox Treasury inspired restrictions to the point where unemployment is substantially above the half-million mark.

    The rigid application of public expenditure cuts — also Treasury inspired — resulting in the postponement of the raising of the school leaving age and the re-introduction of Health Service charges.

    The surrender to anti-trade union prejudices by including the penal clauses in the White Paper on Industrial Relations.

    The failure to dissociate from US policy on Vietnam.

    The attempts to settle the Rhodesian question by means of the 'Tiger' and 'Fearless' proposals.

    The extension of immigration control to the holders of British passports.

    The failure to extend aid to developing countries to reach the moderate and practical target of 1 per cent of gross national product.

    This is not an exhaustive list. I have deliberately excluded some of the wider issues, such as the Common Market, prices and incomes, and defence policy, where the controversies are more complicated. The examples I have mentioned are sufficient to remind us of the all too frequent occasions when large numbers of active Labour Party members have been profoundly disappointed by Government policies. In most of these cases the Labour Party Conference is on record in favour of resolutions contrary to the Government's decisions".

2. Harold Wilson: *The Labour Government: A Personal Record*, Penguin, 1974, p.993.

3. No.11, June 1979, p.4.

4.   A collective work, this was drafted by Allan Flanders and Rita Hinden, editor of *Socialist Commentary*.

5.   *Twentieth Century Socialism*, p.66. An asterisk at this point leads to a defining footnote which says:
     "Full employment cannot, of course, mean zero unemployment. At any moment there will always be some workers unemployed, as they change from one job to another. What is meant is as many vacancies as there are unemployed".

6.   *The Future of Socialism*, Jonathan Cape, 1956, pp.30-31.

7.   Hugh Gaitskell: 'The Economic Aims of the Labour Party' in *The Political Quarterly*, Vol.XIV No.1, January-March 1953, p.10.

8.   J.M. Keynes: *The General Theory of Employment, Interest and Money*. Macmillan, 1936, p.383.

9.   Socialist Union: *Socialism — A New Statement of Principles*, 1952, p.13.

10. R.H. Tawney: *The Radical Tradition*, Penguin Books, 1966, p.177.

11. *The Observer*, 8th July 1979.

CHAPTER TWO

Forward to Yesterday!

Counterpointing the dismal unemployment figures and terrifying economic prognoses, there now flit through the pages of our newspapers ghosts of a former time, in shapes of Roy Jenkins, David Owen and Shirley Williams. Co-architects of significant parts of our present mess, these wraiths now sing out boldly for the merits of yesterday. It is not exactly surprising that yesterday suits them, because it afforded them notable comforts, a certain type of prestige, and a platform from which to denounce tomorrow. They may indeed be right, that tomorrow will be awful. If it is, they will have made an inimitable contribution to that, as well. If it is not, it will be because the working men and women of our country, and those many millions who wish for work but are denied it, have found the way past the beguiling arts of demagogy, and begun to engage directly, on their own account, with the gruelling problems which confront them.

In order to do this, we must not only examine the relationship between unemployment and modern "social democracy". We must also look at the potential for industrial democracy which has suffered so considerably at the hands of self-proclaimed social democrats, and which yet remains our most powerful resource for recovery.

"Between the wars unemployment in Great Britain never fell below 750,000. It averaged 1,650,000 and, for a short time, at the beginning of 1933, it rose to more than 3,000,000. The facts dominated the approach of the Labour Party to home politics during the whole of the period."[1]

That was how Roy Jenkins began his postwar assessment of Labour experience and doctrine in his book *Pursuit of Progress*, published in 1953. But what was the contemporary response to such facts? They were summed up in one book which could represent hundreds of others which appeared in the 'thirties: C.R. Attlee's *The Labour Party in Perspective*. This, Mr Jenkins was to write, a decade and a half later, said "some things which now sound very odd indeed".

"All the major industries" Attlee had assumed when sketching the framework of his future socialist commonwealth, "will be owned and controlled by the community" even while small enterprises could be "carried on individually". There would be significant devolution of power by regional decentralisation. In order to establish speedily effective planning for the creation of work where it was needed, and to produce useful goods which could be more equally distributed, a Labour Government would seek a specific mandate to override opposition from the House of Lords. It would not brook delay in its necessary measures, and would therefore deal more resolutely with the peers than had the Liberals during their constitutional crises, because unlike them, it would be in the business of transforming society.[2]

Attlee was what is today called a "moderate". Much of what Sir Stafford Cripps was writing at the same time would nowadays be regarded as extreme by the majority of the leftwing delegates to Labour Party Conferences. Between Attlee and Cripps the entire Labour Party, by 1937, had come to occupy ground whose topography looks distinctly familiar to those seeking bearings in the nineteen eighties.

With rising three million out-of-work victims already, the Manpower Services Commission informed us in the first half of 1981 that we must expect the numbers to increase still further for at least two more years, and to remain at similar levels for four. The MSC reported also that the direct cost of this profound malaise to the Exchequer had already passed £7 billion annually. This burden takes count solely of taxes forfeited by the revenue and disbursements from social security funds. Assessment of the cost of lost production is more difficult, but cautious estimates put it at not less than £10 billion each year. Other estimates than those of the MSC are higher on all counts.

Unemployment hits hardest at young people, women and black people. The length of exposure to it inevitably increases as the absolute numbers of workless increase. More and more people are deprived of jobs not merely for weeks, but for months and even years. Regional variations add especial burdens in the worst-hit areas. Already there are whole zones of blight, in which entire populations are trapped in profound crisis. Some towns endure percentages of workless people which, if generalised, would imply 5,000,000, even 6,000,000 people on the dole nationally.

Obviously this rot has been perceptibly worse during the decade we entered with Mrs Thatcher than ever it was in the 'thirties years. But it did not begin in 1979.

However, on Labour's front benches nobody admits to kissing hands with the IMF in these more cataclysmic days, as our cities burn and fight. Today, all favour an alternative economic strategy. The next package of proposals which Labour has been discussing under this genial rubric throughout this more recent period is certainly not less measured than was Attlee's book in 1937, to say nothing of the contemporary writings of Strachey or Laski. Yet it is at this moment that Roy Jenkins, Shirley Williams and David Owen, not to speak of David Marquand and a cohort of more pedestrian public figures, have resolved to turn against the Labour movement because of its alleged intransigence and to form a new party based on the cult of moderation. This will uphold, they claim, the principles of social democracy.

Social democracy has, like many other political currents, an ambiguous history. The first English practitioners of the creed were, on the whole, a somewhat pious, not to say tedious bunch of doctrinaires, who formed the Social Democratic Federation around a remarkable eccentric, H.M. Hyndman. They preached a plagiarized and repetitious marxism, not greatly more simpleminded than the cliches of the vigorously traduced Militant Group in the present Labour Party. They were affiliated to the Party for many years, although for most of this time their influence was hardly electric. In Europe, Lenin and Trotsky and Luxemburg and Liebknecht and Kautsky and Bernstein, Pannekoek and Cachin were also social democrats all, until the 1914 war tore the continental Labour movement into warring schisms. But in Britain, Lee and Archbold apart, social democrats only re-emerged as a visible entity in the years after the second world war. Old social democrats sought to extend democratic controls to every aspect of industrial and social life. New social democrats had rather less taxing aspirations. That is why most Labour people still claimed allegiance to one or another variant of "socialism", as did Richard Crossman in 1951, when he tried to explain the Party's worsening electoral fortunes in a characteristically imaginative way:

> "The socialist's greatest achievement is that he has made the working class in this country forget what it felt like to be afraid of unemployment and so become full of the grievances which were previously the monopoly of a prosperous upper class."[3]

This is a poor thought: but in times of intellectual austerity it was rapidly taken up and developed. In its elaboration there arose the school of self-styled social democrats of the later '50s, with which Roy Jenkins himself was closely associated.

Superficially, the establishment of relatively full employment in a predominantly unchanged capitalist economy could be taken as a refutation of Attlee's "socialist objective". Of course, man does not live by bread alone, but moral needs are often more difficult to assert than physical ones. This is no excuse for those of Labour's ideologues who persistently reduced their estimates of their fellows' needs to a mess of pottage. Cutting deeper, Attlee's objectives might have been revised to develop their expressed antipathy to wage-slavery and subordination, as indeed R.H. Tawney suggested, in his last major political essay.

"If a socialist government means business — if it intends to create an economic system socialist all through, and not merely at the top — then it must take the initiative . . . It should use the industries in public ownership as a laboratory where different methods of making industrial democracy a reality are tested . . ."[4]

These were words of good counsel, partly, but only partly, diluted when their author commented:

"there should be a systematic attempt to democratise the practical routine of industrial life by transferring to bodies representing the wage-earners such functions as the allocation of jobs within a working group; the appointment of leaders in charge of them; and matters relating to promotion, dismissal and disciplinary procedures."[5]

In truth this remained a modest programme, but Tawney's self-avowed disciples were almost all persistently deaf to it. For them, all such autonomy in the workforce was contrary to the natural order of things, so that trade unions had to struggle hard, and against relentless official opposition, for even the smallest gains in their members' practical status, whether those in power were "social democrats" or not.

The general lesson drawn from near-full employment by these philosophers was precisely opposed to Tawney's fundamental insight. Since public ownership was for them inconceivable outside the bureaucratic forms imposed under Herbert Morrison's model of the London Passenger Transport Board, then public ownership itself was seen as an electoral liability. Full employment was itself enough, as far as could or should be reached or even attempted in the scale of social transformation. What remained for social democrats was to administer it humanely. Humanity itself became a shrinking concept within this view. Crosland, who was in many ways the most sympathetic of the grouping, nonetheless took Tawney's call for experiments in workplace industrial democracy at their least possible value, and then shrivelled them without mercy:

> "the problem is basically one of "democratic participation" — not however, the mass participation of *all* workers on the *higher* management, but the participation of the *primary* work-group in deciding how its *own* work should be divided, organized and remunerated."[6]

We should notice that Tawney had moved from the general to the particular: from the ideal to a practical proposal. Crosland, by contrast, here starts in the particular, apparently not far from Tawney. But then see how, in his next sentence, he reaches for the general idea:

> "On this view, we must study the enterprise as a social organism, unravel the natural group relationships, *and endeavour to align these with the technological necessities of the work process.*"[7] (my emphasis)

Clearly it is not easy to persuade people that alignment of this kind is an exciting or satisfying mode of life, leave alone a "socialist objective". When they do it to battery hens or veal calves, societies protest about it.

Big Brother is watching you. If Tawney had been listening, he might well have screamed.

Yet Crosland was close to the truth, in a limited way, as well as the consensus of his time when he spoke of "the sellers' market for labour" which full employment created, as transferring a degree of effective social power to working people.

This was the shared conviction of all the social democrats of the revisionist vintage, whether, like Douglas Jay, they were to remain part of the Labour movement, or like Roy Jenkins, they were to set up in opposition to it. Sadly, it was not a conviction strong enough to prevent them from ulcerating their stomachs in the cause of reducing or subverting that power, whenever they were to come to office in the Wilson and subsequent Callaghan administrations. Denied any democratic conquests of industrial significance, workpeople used their "sellers' market", such as it was, to maximise their earnings. They were thus identified as inflationary pressurisers, so that every governmental ingenuity must be deployed to curb their exploitation of such advantages as they might otherwise have derived from this market.

Happily, such curbs worked far from perfectly, and the reason was that while full employment made less fundamental changes than could easily have been achieved in the organisation of work, it did greatly strengthen and consolidate some of the processes of political democracy. In this context it wrested serious advances on public welfare, and paradoxically went a long way towards giving the moral social democratic platform of "Butskellism" as it became called, the semblance of justification.

Yet these gains were all allowed to slide into jeopardy when the 1974-9 Labour Governments chose a series of policy options which reneged upon the "first and foremost" priority of *Twentieth Century Socialism*, flouting the "first condition of a socialist economy" and thus entering into "a disgraceful exchange".[8] Mr Jenkins and his three co-responsible companions can have it one way: if the Labour Government made such a "disgraceful exchange" with conscious forethought then it was reneging on that very social democracy which they claim as their tradition. Or they can have it another way, protesting their lack of any such villainy, and claiming that vast impersonal economic convulsions deprived them of any choice in the matter. In this case, they are claiming that the social conditions which gave rise to social democracy have disappeared. If this be so, then the relevance of the doctrine has also disappeared. In fact, they seem to make a third claim, which is that social democracy is to do with abstract moderation, and that by implication Flanders, Crosland, Hinden and everyone else were totally unjustified in linking it to such impolite matters as the right to work. Some people still think that to be moderate in the face of rank injustice is an ignoble response, but no doubt there are persons in Oxford or at the BBC who will explain to them that it is necessary to maintain an impartial detachment between good and evil. Naturally, such matters are not discussed very loudly in social democratic meetings. Instead, there are lusty invocations on the merits of yesterday. And yes, yesterday was more comfortable than today.

Certainly, if we could go back, three million workless people would opt like a shot for the apparent stability of the full employment years, however little they might offer in spiritual fulfilment and human dignity. It is an impossible "if", though. There is no going back. Far from moving into industrial (and therefore also "social") democracy, we shall quickly see our political freedoms shredded if full employment is not restored. And the old consensus cannot even promise to halve the queues at the Labour Exchanges, leave alone remove them. It is not at all excluded that it will increase them. As a result, tensions rise, old and young come into bitter conflict, racial disharmony becomes more sinister, the police are armed with C.S. gas, and authoritarian trends become daily more ominous.

De-industrialisation, the collapse of one sector after another of manufacturing industry, has reached epidemic proportions. More and more equipment is sold at a tithe of its value to competitors overseas, as the liquidators work overtime. Recovery recedes with every sale.

Against all this, the social democrats of all parties offer no hope. Not only of them has offered any beginning of a plausible suggestion about how to restore full employment. Reflation alone will suck in vast imports from the EEC whilst only marginally admitting industrial growth. Protection is still abjured, leave alone the planning of trade, which is the only rational response. The spokesmen of the old order, whether they sport new colours or not, are all tacitly united in assuming permanent mass unemployment. This means civil dislocation and stress at unbearable levels, and it can only be policed by the abandonment of every liberal precept which has been established in the postwar era. And at the end of it all, open bankruptcy. It is not imaginable that the British people will tolerate this dreadful prospectus, when they understand it for what it really is.

Footnotes

1. Roy Jenkins: *Pursuit of Progress — A critical analysis of the achievement and prospect of the Labour Party*, Heinemann, 1953, p.55.
2. C.R. Attlee: *The Labour Party in Perspective*, Gollancz (Left Book Club), 1937, p.153 *et seq.*
3. R.H.S. Crossman: *Socialist Values in a Changing Situation*, Fabian Tract No.286, 1951.
4. R.H. Tawney: *The Radical Tradition*, Penguin Books, 1966, p.185.
5. *Ibid.*, p.186.
6. C.A.R. Crosland: "What the Worker Wants", *Encounter*, February 1959, p.17.
7. *Ibid.*
8. Allan Flanders and Rita Hinden: *Twentieth Century Socialism*, Penguin Books, 1956, p.66.

CHAPTER THREE

Doctor Jekyll
and the Rt. Hon. Mr. Hyde

I have a good deal of personal feeling for David Owen. He is an abrasive character, but he takes ideas more seriously than some of his associates. My guess is that during his last weekend in the Labour Party he felt pretty much like I felt on the day they expelled me, in November 1965. Watching him on television in the reports on Labour's Special Conference, he seemed a good deal less relaxed and more haggard than the self-possessed young politician whose picture appears on the dust-jacket of his book. Sometimes it is hard work being in a minority, and no doubt it is even more difficult when you have finished being Foreign Secretary.

And yet David Owen has not yet been expelled from anything, and a good deal of his present all-too-apparent anguish comes from his own very arbitrary choice to set his course on departure from the Labour Party. His book* will be, and should be, widely read, because it is clearly intended as a manifesto for this separation. While it would have been far better for us to discuss its themes within the same Party, we must be quite sure that we never make the mistake of the old Wilson-Jenkins Establishment, of refusing to address such oppositional ideas directly. We must discuss these writings even if their originator does disruptive things. Not only should we follow this argument through, but we must also be careful in doing so to seek truth, the more so when many passions are being raised by quite inexcusable behaviour.

As for the platform of the coming splitlet, it does not rest on any foundation of principle, and it will founder for this reason, which has two aspects.

First, David Owen's book could not in conscience be signed by the

*Face the Future, David Owen, Jonathan Cape.

closest of his collaborators in the new formation he is launching. They don't agree with one another. His arguments for industrial democracy in Chapter 12 cut the feet from under Shirley Williams, who personally organized the death by a thousand cuts which was inflicted on the Bullock Report. Flawed as this was, there was nothing left of it when Shirley Williams' cabinet committee had done with it. Neither was there any alternative constructive proposal. His arguments for equality, in Part Two, undermine another colleague. Fond though he is of the appellations, no-one could describe bon viveur, merchant banker and European Commissioner Jenkins as fraternal, leave alone equalitarian. As for the regrettable Bill "Atlantic" Rogers, he is simply a failed apparachik, and his own pamphlet against nuclear disarmament has none of the subtlety, nuance and yes, sensitivity, of David Owen's writing on the same theme in Chapter 19 of this book. These are the subjects of three chapters to start with, and the three other cavaliers could only endorse them if they were willing to add hypocrisy to perjury. The basis for the unity of these persons may indeed rest in a shared fondness for moderation, but there is no discernable record of practical commitment, even "moderate" commitment, on Doctor Owen's chosen issues.

Second, the disagreements with the parent body are not clearly or fairly stated. It isn't at all plain what they actually are. When we examine this rather long book in its own right, we find that in it David Owen is really trying on all sorts of other people's clothes. He has tried on Tony Benn's commitment against corporatism, that of the IWC and others to workers' control and industrial democracy, odd socks from various ecologists and conservationists, and a big covering cape of "decentralisation" which owes something to all of us, as well as our predecessors. Few of these are acknowledged, because it seems that David Owen has not read very deeply into his sources. Those who are cited include William Morris, G.D.H. Cole and R.H. Tawney, all of whom are patron saints of the modern workers' control movement, and would as soon join Al Capone as a secessionist gang of three. Even their bones would kick against such an involuntary co-option. Yet in his partial endorsement of local democracy, David Owen reveals a concern which is far more widely shared on the left of the Labour Party than elsewhere.

Of course, this is not to say that the mix of pious thoughts here outlined stands up as a programme. If small is beautiful, big is presently in command, and to defeat big today requires a strong and co-ordinated oppositional strategy. Transnational companies and a host of non-democratic international powers positively require a countervailing internationalism based on the convergence of democratic forces, against which, in the last analysis, this book takes its own strong stand. I shall discuss this aspect of the Owen argument below. Of course, in any discussion of plan and market, today's prescriptions require a shifting mix of policies which extend the one and limit the other. But this no more implies rigid centralism than it implies a return to rural handicrafts. It is one thing to discuss long term trends in the mix, and quite another to consider immediate practical options within those trends. To liberate extensive co-operative production requires a major shift in economic power relations, without which the untrammeled operation of the present monopolised semi-market will choke most little experiments in co-operation stone dead, just as it already daily chokes existing small businesses. To develop effective local municipal enterprise against the grain requires similar sympathetic central intervention. To speak of varieties of common ownership, then, only makes sense when we are prepared to confront irresponsible and highly centralised industrial and economic power, and not in the least when we seek at all costs to appease it. The big industrial powers are willing to endorse near-bankrupt co-ops which offer them no challenges but they fear thriving self-management more than sinful bishops dread a whole plague of devils.

Is decentralisation wrong, then? Not at all. What the Labour movement faces in the run-up to the next election is a real level of unemployment between three and four million. No serious politician thinks that any amount of central initiative, state or otherwise, can restore full employment in any measurable time, now that the task has become so daunting. Since it takes several years to get capital-intensive large enterprises from the blueprint stage to production, an adequate central answering strategy would be quite beyond the effective reach of any Labour Government. Yet the restoration of full employment is the priority of all priorities. That is why more and more labour groups seek to find ways to create local enterprise, including co-ops and direct municipal producer groups. Obviously, to think this is likely to work in the absence of a simultaneous shift in central political and economic power is to pray for the triumph of good works over all available evidence.

Evidence is, however, not Dr. Owen's strongest suit. "It is the bureaucratic centralisers, the corporatists, who now dominate British socialism and their influence, far from being checked, is growing" he tells us. He also revives an old fabian prediction that British socialism would ultimately divide into "a collective party supporting a strong central administration and a counterbalancing anarchist party defending individual initiative against that administration."

There may indeed be such parties, but they reflect a division inside each of us, David Owen and myself not excluded, so that a polarisation into separate forces is misguided, to put it kindly. The tension between centralism, without which democratic control is just as impossible as autocratic control; and individual initiative, without which any society is flattened into dead conformity, is continuing and persistent. To quote such revisionist writers as Kolakowski without appreciating this is to do them the injustice of ignoring the truest things they have said. In the same way, the socialist impulse to planning is in constant tension with the socialist principle of self-management, and unless the dialogue between the two is institutionally combined in one determining forum, with real interchange and flux, then both are separated into a dreadful pair of warring half-truths. That his own half-truth has now got hold of David Owen is no excuse for letting its mirror reflection dominate us.

And the half-truth *is* in charge over there. In what way is, for example, Tony Benn a "centraliser" or a "corporatist"? He fought both the civil service and his cabinet colleagues in order to establish the new workers' co-ops, without which the subsequent developments which interest David Owen could never have taken place. He opposed the institutions of patronage which have hitherto centralised political power in the hands of prime ministers, thus making possible a rejuvenation of the Labour Party in the country and of the individual members' role in Parliament itself. He has spoken and worked most vigorously against quangos as a pre-eminent governmental form, and struggled against overwhelming odds to encourage the widest range of forms of community organization and local voluntary activity. The Lucas Aerospace shop stewards began work on their alternative plan at his suggestion, and David Owen was nowhere in sight when the Labour Government went persistently deaf to the results, which were the most audacious, enterprising and exciting initiatives by any group of ordinary workers for many years. It was the "centralising" Labour Party Conference which supported these trade unionists, much to the embarrassment of the Parliamentary leadership.

Is the quarrel all a misunderstanding, then? Not at all. David Owen's book has created an imaginary Labour Party, hell-bent on bringing Bulgarian political habits to Albion's shores. This fiction has a clear political meaning, and it is obviously hostile to labour. It is also hostile to any practical prospect of reform. Real decentralised initiative positively requires an appropriate central strategy, since the one defines itself in relation to the other. David Owen's decentralisation is the watchword of a hollow programme. It will attract, perhaps, the support of a previous generation of hollow men, dignatories such as Lord Robens, Lord Marsh, Lord George Brown and the rest of them. The mass baptism of such converted sinners, who really were the architects, along with Roy Jenkins, of much of the "corporatism" which David Owen now belatedly denounces, will be a thing to watch. Don't be surprised if the holy water boils, with so much wickedness to wash away.

It seems clear that we shall be able to cope with this challenge, however hard the media works for it. David Owen will discover it more difficult. Probably his Dr. Jekyll half will find such supporters as his Mr. Hyde soul is able to recruit most tiresome, and soon become lonely for his former colleagues. But be that as it may, the argument to which he invites us will, if we allow ourselves to disregard the personal loss, be a great help to us, in that it will help us both to refine our answering response and win ever wider support.

*   *   *

David Owen's international perspectives begin with his admiration of the achievements of four major European socialist Parties: the Swedes, the Austrians, the Dutch and the Germans. Originally, he tells us, he wanted to describe himself as a democratic socialist. Unfortunately, the British Labour Party is generally seen as typical of "democratic socialist" organizations, the more so since it began to steer leftwards as a result of its unpleasant experiences in the late 'sixties and 'seventies. It is his rejection of the trend in the Labour Party, which brings Dr Owen to accept, with his continental inspirers, the title of "social democrat", which, he says, has become "a description of . . . a socialist who worked constructively within the framework of a mixed economy" rather than against it. The Polish philosopher, Kolakowski, gives Dr. Owen his watchword for this process: "an obstinate will to erode by inches" which he counterposes to an unrealistic will "to jump by miles".

Let us look at this for a moment. With 2.4 million unemployed in Britain at the time of writing, three million by Christmas, and more to come, is the erosion of unemployment to be done "by inches"? The foundation stone of British revisionism, like that of much continental social-democratic thinking, was that permanent full employment through the application of Keynesian techniques had made a large part of the old socialist prescription unnecessary. The refutation of this error, for a long time quite plausible, has not come "by inches", but, thanks to Denis Healey and others, first by furlongs, then by miles, and now, under Mrs. Thatcher, by leagues and leagues. No Party which existed to defend the interests of working people could accept that this condition should be regarded as permanent. Quite outside the fields of doctrine, urgent action is required to produce a rapid and drastic improvement, and the restoration of full employment is a basic condition for the defence of what liberal-minded people in Britain regard as a free society. The degree of "mix" in the mixed economy will rightly be judged in relation to its effect on this outcome.

Without entering into a close consideration of the European models which David Owen has chosen, it is obvious that each of them has encountered different employment problems, and none will be able to ignore the challenge already faced here in this country, if their unemployment reaches our levels. Already the Austrians have a greatly larger conventional and bureaucratic public sector than we do, and all the other three parties are markedly more "corporatist" than is the Labour Party. David Owen's platform would attract little support in any of them, so that the same inducements would cause him to split from us would also invite him to divide from them. Yet it is not in this area, but in the field of international relations that Dr. Owen's models most sharply reveal their rejection of his assumptions. He, for his part, tries to be a loyal Atlanticist, if not, like William Rogers, a chorister of NATO uber alles. His chosen European models, for their part, reveal themselves rather deaf to such music. Unlike this David, many of them are to a greater or lesser extent *opposed* to Goliath, East or West.

Austria is neutral by four-power agreement, and under the politics of spheres of influence which disgraced the postwar settlement, each of those powers has a treaty right to intervene if Austrian policies change in this respect. Sweden is neutral by choice, and Olof Palme has followed a determined policy of opposition to imperialism and interventionism. Soon after Harold Wilson visited Prague to tell Mr. Husak that we must "let bygones be bygones", Palme made a forthright speech in which he compared the Czechoslovak quisling with Vietnamese Marshal Kao Ky. Palme was the first statesman in Europe to call for a nuclear-free zone in all Europe, banishing atomic weapons from the whole continent. His powerful speech to the Socialist International in Helsinki in 1978 resulted in the setting up of a commission which has provided that body with a far-reaching policy statement, approved in Madrid in November 1980, committing the whole movement to this policy as an ultimate goal. The Commission was led by the Finn Kalevi Sorsa and the Austrian Walter Hacker, both of whom have endorsed the

Russell Foundation's European Nuclear Disarmament appeal. This appeal also has won the support of key leaders of the Dutch Labour Party. The trend of the majority of David Owen's alleged "major influences", then, is towards resistance to the arms race, agreed continental denuclearisation, and a consequent transformation of the two super-power blocs. Their ultimate goal would be quite compatible with the non-alignment of all Europe. It would also be compatible with the present committment of the overwhelming majority of the Labour Party. However, it is this commitment which has, to use Denis Healey's inelegant phrase, persuaded Mr. Rogers that now "sod off day" has arrived.

But none of this quite fits the perspectives of *Facing the Future*. David Owen is a humane man, and he knows enough about the horrors of the present runaway arms race to take up a significantly different stand from that of William Rogers, whose peace policy consists of adroitly saying whatever the US State Department said yesterday, only more crudely. (Mr. Rogers is going to have problems in the epoch of President Reagan. Or perhaps he isn't?) Dr. Owen half welcomes protest and specifically endorses Lord Mountbatten's and Lord Zuckerman's condemnation of the strategy for a European "Theatre" limited nuclear war, which apparently poses no problems whatever for his temporary co-adjutant. Limited war is official NATO policy, so it has never crossed Mr. Rogers' mind to question it. That Dr. Owen supports its most distinguished critics is an indication of profound divergences to come within the gang of three, four or two dozen, however many they may ultimately become. Even if they made twenty-seven recruits, they would soon be two gangs, not one.

Having said that, I must add that David Owen has quite misread the message of European Nuclear Disarmament, when he claims that its advocates "despair of disarmament by negotiation". On the contrary, they are precisely the people who wish such negotiations to begin, on a number of related levels. What do merit despair are the present intentions of the super-powers, who were rightly and almost unanimously condemned (as also was Great Britain) by the nations involved in the Non-Proliferation Review Conference in Geneva in August, 1980, because they have for years talked vacuously about disarmament whilst at the same time escalating their expenditure on war-preparations to the point of mania. Against this we pose the need for a policy shift "of miles", which we seek to approach, if not "by inches", at any rate by rapid and practical steps.

For umpteen years the Swedes (in the Unden Plan and thereafter) have vainly argued for a Baltic nuclear-free zone, and have constantly been frustrated by the Norwegians, who belonged to NATO. The Norwegian nuclear disarmament movement, however, once it gathered mass support, after the decision to install new NATO "theatre" missiles, was able to give us all a magnificent Christmas present. Under pressure, their Prime Minister has now agreed that Norway also will now work for the creation of such a zone. We won this significant victory in less than a year. What has David Owen, by contrast, got to show for all his time in the foreign office?

The general goal of continental nuclear disarmament succeeds because it provides a framework for both protest *and* negotiations. It permits a wide variety of intermediary objectives: lesser nuclear-free zones, jigsawing into greater ones; various categories of arms limitation, and the restriction of particular weaponry; agreed phased reductions of overall armament: all are thinkable when millions of people begin to express their concern. But none have any meaning as purely diplomatic proposals. The first breakthrough in Norway confirms that our broad strategy will work. As it develops, will David Owen be able to maintain his opposition to it? Perhaps this is an open question. On the evidence of this book, he might not. But on the evidence of their professed policies his colleagues will fight it every inch of the way.

CHAPTER FOUR

Death and Decay All Around

Stephen Haseler[1] thinks that British social democracy is about to expire, unless a rather improbably vague consensus can emerge to contain Marxist pressures and prevent the installation of a siege economy run by central command. David Howell[2] thinks that social democracy is already dead, or at any rate decayed beyond genuine remedy. Both have produced elegant arguments in support of their theses, but neither carries real conviction.

The most serious problem involved in both works is that such concepts as "social democracy" are rather empty of precise meaning. Haseler's favourite ideologues are Tony Crosland and the late John Strachey, who, before his own voyage to Damascus was just about as orthodox a member of the Muscovite confession as one could hope to meet. Strachey's conversion was surely evidence that the boundary of doctrine is less inflexible than Haseler seems to think and that live issues are bound to burst through, even in the most unlikely minds.

At the same time, Haseler venerates Orwell as a prepopulist forerunner of his own school, without in any way meeting his radicalism, which earned him the uncomfortable vignette of Trotskyist at a time when the popes of conventional social democracy, Sidney and Beatrice Webb, were celebrating the world of the great purges and Gulag as "a new civilisation". When Strachey fell out with this world, he (and a large part of the rest of the leaders of European socialism) then became almost equally uncritical admirers of the American establishment.

Almost alone in the postwar British Labour Party, Aneurin Bevan sought from the beginning to reverse this new dependence, and in a remarkable campaign he almost dragged his colleagues into a measure of autonomy, by his advocacy of open relations with People's China.

David Howell completely underestimates the significance of all this, while Stephen Haseler has no approving words for any of it. Neither can he face the fact that, as a result of Bevan's failure, the problem of socialist democracy in Britain still hinges upon the need to create an autonomous European Socialism.

Haseler remains, for a "radical revisionist", the littlest of little Englanders. That is why he is so pessimistic, because he fails to see that within the wider area of manoeuvre of European labour, a whole variety of democratic strategies become possible, including some which are by no means "anti-parliamentary".

But all must involve fierce efforts towards the democratisation of industry and economic decision-taking, towards the extension of genuine popular checks upon bureaucratic institutions, and towards the further separation of powers throughout industry and society involving significant increases in democratic accountability.

These calls are to be heard all the way from Brindisi to Bergen. If they are "populism", then so be it. Are they social-democracy? They may well be, but they might almost equally be Italian communism, or what Haseler regards as Utopianism, or "syndicalism" in the current swear-vocabulary, or even, dreadful though it may sound, "Marxism".

One thing they are not, though, and that is dead or even dying.

When David Howell is analysing the fate of "moderates" in British trade unions, he nearly gets his finger on the underlying trend of our times. He points out that "postal ballots for seats on the engineers' executive have been accompanied by widespread media publicity and have resulted in impressive moderate victories."

But he then flies past the real question this poses, to ask how far such responses "will survive continuous economic pressures"? What is profoundly important about this case-history is surely that the Scanlon ascendancy came about as a democratic rebellion against the domination of a clique which repeatedly over-rode highly specific instructions and mandates arrived at by the union's elected representative assemblies.

And when did Scanlon's formidable alliance begin to lose? Not while the economy came good, but precisely when it found itself defending the practice of (less than 10 per cent) branch ballots against the institution of postal ballots involving a third or so of the membership.

Of course, the Left has a point when it complains about outside interference in such ballots; but it will not win again until it regains the democratic initiative by espousing the idea of 70 per cent or 80 per cent factory ballots, which will imply a reorganisation of the union's anachronistic structure.[3] If this is true, engineers are like Scotsmen and victims of road development, in that they want more direct say in the governance of their affairs. And don't we all?

Whether this means the death of social-democracy or not is a problem of rather silly labels. If it does, it also very likely means the death of Western European "communism" in the sense that this itself is becoming, wherever Communists dispose of large popular support, very largely another label. Berlinguer can't lead his masses where they don't want to go.

Stephen Haseler doesn't see things this way, because he reacts like his mirror-image in the beleagured old-guard of the other Left-wing hierarchy. Carron was "his" man, so his behaviour was always by definition right, even when it was anything but democratic. But we may be confident that the last quarter of our century will be a hard time for all such apparachiks, and that is not the least reason for holding fast to the notion that both socialism and democracy have hardly yet started on their long future evolution.

1. *The Death of British Democracy*, by Stephen Haseler (Elek, £5.95).
2. *British Social Democracy*, by David Howell (Croom Helm, £6.95).
3. More recent union postal ballots have shown a marked fall in the proportion of the membership which registers a vote. If this trend continues, the postal system will soon show little better results than its predecessor.

CHAPTER FIVE

Dwindling Resources

Shirley Williams begins her book* with a confession: she has, she says, been too busy to think for some time, because, as a minister "one lives on the dwindling resources of past reading and past thinking".

True, she has been on a crash course since her defeat at Stevenage, both at Harvard and at the Policy Studies Institute in London. Yet she still has some way to travel, before she re-enters the modern world. She might have been better off at Ruskin College, because there she would have been faced with some salient facts about the present structure of the capitalism which she wishes to maintain (albeit in a "mix" the consistency of which is not entirely clear). I do not mean to be snide. Quite seriously, there is an important body of contemporary socialist writing of which Shirley Williams is simply unaware.

Early, she informs us that she understands that "the house that Keynes built has now largely been destroyed". How? It was undermined, she tells us, by the economic effects of the Vietnam war, the turpitude of western governments in allowing bodies like the IMF, the World Bank and GATT to remain unresponsive to the needs of the third world, and by the oil price crisis.

But this listing of causes leaves out of account the major reason for the collapse of the international Keynesian framework, which is the growth of the power and influence of transnational corporations. By the seventies, one third of British foreign trade (and more of US trade) took place internally within subsidiaries of such companies. These, in pursuit of their direct interests, played the exchanges systematically, both to exploit differential national interest rates and, when relevant, to husband their liquid resources.

Such massive manipulation provoked a rapidly increasing trend of devaluations and revaluations, and a dutch auction of interest rates,

*Politics is for People by Shirley Williams; Allen Lane £8.50 and Penguin £2.50.

culminating in the American dollar crisis of 1971, which marked the effective end of the Keynesian world system.

Every other contributory element cited by Shirley Williams can only be weighed in relation to its effects on this structural relationship, which does not appear in *Politics is for People*. Economics, it is plain, is not for some people. Multinational corporations are entirely absent from the power system described in this book. They are mentioned four times in all: to tell us that they are not centred on improving the quality of life, to tell us they exist, to explain that they make nations interdependent, and to complain that the EEC code of conduct for such corporations has been little invoked in Britain.

Really, this amounts to more than an omission: it either betokens a degree of ignorance which would be surprising even in a busy minister, or, what would be even more remarkable, an actual suppression. No one can write a modern politics which stands up to even cursory analysis without focusing upon the growth of the transnationals' arbitrary power as a fact of central importance.

As it is, Shirley Williams skitters like a delicate pond-fly over the surface of her subject, writing gracefully about how each and all should be fraternal to one another, pirouetting here for the ecologists, there for the third world, but never beginning to engage with the deep realities which make actual political action either feasible or impossible. Hamlet without the Prince, this book does not even give us Rosencrantz or Guildenstern's view of the Court, for at least they saw what was going on around them.

A melody of fashionable echoes, her chapters do indirectly reflect part of the contemporary argument. "Small is beautiful" is a radical insight. But in Shirley Williams' interpretation, this becomes "less concentration"; first in industry, then in public service. Some industries are "better" than others, we are told. They export more, or are more profitable. But which are transnational, and how far is the "effective" sector dominated by multinationals? The question does not occur, so no answers are even contemplated. All this reduces the book's treatment of unemployment, the central problem of our time, to triviality. She betrays no comprehension of the severity of the collapse of British manufacturing industry, nor any glimmer of understanding of the vast task involved in restoring full employment.

The truth is that the collapse of the slum sector of the British economy further shifts power towards the transnationals, which makes the recovery of employment greatly more difficult.

She is canny enough to refrain from making any promises about this: it is absolutely clear that her programme would entail the permanent continuance of unemployment at or above present levels. The convenient libel about this condition, that it is an "act of God", is not an easy one for a professed Christian to invoke. These failures of perception combine to form the false polarities within which Shirley Williams sets her argument. Because the real power in today's world is not considered, her book has more room for rather simplistic ideology.

On the one side, Thatcher rampant: on the other that Bulgarian Labour left, bent upon nationalising everything that breathes and poking its poisoned umbrella ferrules into every dissentient thinker. Of course, this is a travesty, and to give her credit, Shirley Williams knows it to be such. No leading figure in the Labour movement holds the views which have here been compounded together from one eccentricity or another, liberally mixed with straw. If she wishes to get to grips with her serious Labour adversaries, I will set her some homework. Let her take Stuart Holland's *The Socialist Challenge* and respond to it, section by section. Then we shall get an honest statement of an honest disagreement.

Nowhere do the implications of polemic rhetoric have more baleful results than in this book's discussion of industrial democracy.

Shirley Williams chaired the cabinet sub-committee which was charged with the task of gutting the Bullock report. She went at it until nothing, but nothing, was left. The original proposals had been rather modest. The 1979 white paper, however, was a retreat to a point far behind the original tentative beginnings which had been essayed all those years before. Yet splendid words conclude her chapter 9: "This one reform could bring in its wake a long-delayed rejuvenation. We should not be daunted by the difficulties, but rather invigorated by the possibilities." However, when she held direct responsibility for this "possibility", little though her vigour may have been, the amount of daunting required to inhibit her was even less. On her record, it seems clear that the very last thing Shirley Williams will ever promote will be democracy in factories.

This book traces a sad story. Democracy in Britain faces a bleak and difficult struggle. Britain's crisis of deindustrialisation may indeed also see the collapse of her democratic powers, all of which are under ferocious attack from the same establishment which will praise this rather feeble book as a worthy successor to those of Hobbes and

Locke.

The Labour Party is now embattled in the most crucial task of its history, to develop and deepen democratic institutions in order to find ways to recover work and hope for our people. To defect from this struggle was bad enough. To defect from the effort to understand and explain how such a struggle has become necessary, as this tract has done, is probably worse.

CHAPTER SIX

Industrial Democracy
& Nationalisation

In the last conference which it held during the Second World War, the Labour Party resolved upon a radical programme of nationalization. This was carried against concerted platform opposition. After the 1945 Election, the Attlee administration implemented this programme. Coal, railways, gas, electricity, road haulage, iron and steel, all came under public ownership.

Nationalization had become a catchword of the left, although, like many other catchwords, it was not very precise in its meaning. Certainly there is evidence that different people nourished very diverse expectations, whilst joining together to welcome the new reforms. Syndicalists had lost much of their sharpness, but still expected that public ownership would enlarge the area of industrial democracy. State socialists, by contrast, were interested in macro economic decision making, and even the Fabians tended to accept what the Webbs called the "vocation of leadership", which they saw as emergent in the institutions of the Soviet Union, but which others identified with English middle class virtue. From the left, John Strachey, for instance, argued in favour of "planned production for community consumption" very much in the tradition of the Webbs. For him, "the master question (was) whether the occurrence of crisis is accidental to or inherent in the capitalist system". If crises were accidental, "then we should certainly work for their gradual elimination by appropriate reforms. For who would be so mad as to recommend the scrapping of the system itself if the catastrophes which it is bringing upon us were remediable". Indeed, in the same very popular book *The Nature of Capitalist Crisis*, Strachey wrote "if it were true . . . that the Fascists are the agents of a separate class, able to set up a workable economic system, which would end the present chronic state of crisis . . . then there would be a great deal to be said for the fascists."[1]

This train of thought probably helped Strachey in his later years to adapt to Keynes, and certainly helped postwar Labour Governments to see the benefits of nationalisation as mainly administrative. Old and bankrupt industries were bought out, and extensively modernized at Government expense. The compensation payable for them gave a new lease of power to private capitalism, enabling those whose resources had hitherto been locked in a stagnant sector to voyage out in search of new more profitable investment. At the same time, the enlarged public sector certainly constituted a useful management lever for would-be economic planners.

All of these public industries were brought under control of boards appointed by an appropriate minister, modelled on the scheme worked out for London Transport during the 1930s by Herbert Morrison. There was no direct worker representation on them, although a limited number of trade union functionaries were offered positions when the new boards were constituted. These persons were expected to sever their direct trade union connections and were in no way held accountable to their former memberships. It is not accidental that Morrison had justified his model of public enterprise by reference to management patterns in the Soviet Union.[2]

The effect of all this was not entirely unpredictable, because in 1944 the TUC had agreed an *Interim Report on Postwar Reconstruction* which had been drafted in consultation with the Labour Party's Executive, and which proposed to introduce worker participation in the control of private industry while opposing it in the public sector. Management in this section was to be chosen for its "competence efficiently to administer" and the resultant boards would answer to the public through their relevant ministers "responsible to Parliament". Again and again Governmental spokesmen took their stand on this principle, even though it soon became clear that the actual degree of public accountability offered by the Morrison form of nationalisation was dilute indeed. Answering a Labour Party debate in 1946, Emmanuel Shinwell, the Minister for Mines, insisted that the "first principle" of the new National Coal Board must be "that we employ the best men for the job".[3] Sir Stafford Cripps went further, insisting that "there is not as yet a very large body of workers in Britain capable of taking over large enterprises". "I think", he told his constituents in Bristol in October 1946, "it would be almost impossible to have worker-controlled industry in Britain, even if it were on the whole desirable."[4]

This view was widely criticised. Indeed, there was some basis for such criticism in the same 1944 *Interim Report* which was so widely cited in evidence for the agreed need for professional expertise in public enterprise management. This Report had also laid down the principle that efficiency also required that policy should "be subject to the continuous influence of those whom it directly affects". Coal was the first industry to be taken over, because the industry had become a symbol of the evils of capitalist exploitation. The miners, whose original demands for nationalisation had been heavily stamped with the imprint of syndicalist and guild socialist ideas, were divided by the new institutions designed for them, much though they welcomed nationalisation in principle. Both Labour Party activists and the communist opposition within the NUM reflected this division. Some communists joined the Regional Coal Boards as appointed members, and some declined invitations. George Brown, then a young Labour back-bencher for the mining division of Belper, made a passionate speech during the Nationalisation debate, insisting that "we shall cause the greatest disappointment to very many miners if we are not very careful about which people we take into the management of this new industry". He cited a plea from one of his constituents "Let us have no well-feathered nests for the tyrants of the past". This judgement, he reported, "very well expresses what is in the minds of the men".[5] But Mr. Shinwell, from his ministerial desk, claimed that he "had to start on a clear desk", to elaborate the Nationalisation Act, in the implementation of which the communist Miners' leader, Arthur Horner "never put the ideological precepts of his . . . affiliations before the welfare of the men he represented".[6] Whatever individual communists thought of the Coal Board, it was not until 1948, after the launching of the Marshall Plan and the outbreak of a visible cold war, that Harry Pollitt published a pamphlet demanding workers' direct representation.[7]

There were no fewer arguments in other industries, where the traditions of some of the unions were even less tractable than those of the NUM. The Railways were precipitated into a major debate. Unlike the miners, the railwaymen had their own weekly newspaper, the *Railway Review*. During the three years from 1946 on, "hundreds of yards of column space were taken up by articles and correspondence on the subject of workers' control".[8] Immediately after the 1945 election results had been declared, the NUR's annual general meeting unanimously resolved that "workers' participation . . . is an indispensable requisite to ensure the success of a publicly owned transport industry". Those officials who sought to justify the Labour Party's managerialist approach to nationalisation were wont to cite the fact that "the trade unions did not control the railways in Russia", thus echoing Mr. Herbert Morrison's own defence of his model for public ownership of industry, a decade earlier, during the debates which shaped Labour policy in the prewar years. Mr James Figgins, the postwar General Secretary of the union, stood with his rank-and-file on this matter: workers' control, he said, "may have failed in the co-operative movement, but I am perfectly certain that we in the railway industry will not fail to solve the problem, because I know of no industry in this country where men have to display greater initiative".[9]

The railwaymen remained obdurate, and in 1949 they were still insisting on "50 percent workers' representation at all levels". This commitment was shared by the postmen, whose union had always defended the perspectives of guild socialism, and continued to do so until well into the 1960s. Evaluating these and other similar responses to nationalisation, Eireen White, MP, concluded in a 1951 fabian survey of the field, that "the issue of workers' representation is by no means dead".[10] Dissatisfaction about the exclusion of directly elected worker representatives concerned only a minority, if a significant one: but there was also much more general dissatisfaction, even within the given Morrisonian framework, about the inadequate number of appointments given to trade unionists. In 1948 the TUC was informed, during Congress, that out of 46 Coal Board Divisional appointments, only nine had been made from the unions; that the Transport Commission had one trade unionist only among its five members and the Railway Executive one out of seven. Complaints brought no perceptible change, and in 1951 the total of union appointees on national and regional boards numbered 44 out of some 350. At the same time, seven General Councillors were among the 44, and Citrine passed through the NCB to be chosen as Chairman of the Central Electricity Authority.

Union members who received such appointments were often placed on the boards of industries in which they had no practical experience, and the Bank Clerks complained that they were not even consulted when one member of the General Council was given a place on the Court of the Bank of England. With the return of a Conservative administration in 1951, trade union appointments were continued, but they had already lost any semblance of representativity, and increasingly frequently provoked adverse commentary among rank-and-file union members. This began to find insistent echoes among the more radical trade union leaders through the later 1950s, as is perfectly exemplified by Clive Jenkins' indictment of Labour Party policy in respect of public corporations, published in *The Insiders*, a pamphlet issued by *Universities and Left Review* in 1958. Five employee rights were itemised in this influential tract:

"1. Workers in an industry are entitled to a voice in workshop management and in higher policy making.

2. Their authority at local level should be absolute in such questions as working arrangements, hiring and dismissals.

3. They should be allowed to select their own supervisors (providing these are technically qualified).

4. Workers' representatives should sit on the Managing Board for their industry.

5. This scheme of sharing in power (while operated by the joint union organizations within the corporations) should be manned by employees only and *not* full-time trade union officers, who should remain primarily responsible for the negotiation of wages, conditions, and grievance settling. . . ."[11]

The main concession to "participation" in the different nationalisation acts was the agreement to write provisions for joint consultation into them. Consultation was always seen by those in office as an advisory process, although its capacity to involve workers varied with the necessary degree of ambiguity which the device incorporated in its structure. As was the case in Engineering, also in Mining, Joint Production Committees had flourished during the war, as part of the drive for war production. Communist support for them was broadly continued in the immediate postwar period. In fact, left-wingers were as divided as the right, and frequently "participated" with much enthusiasm. Yet gradually support for consultation fell away, even in the mining industry.

Indeed, the fact that colliery consultative committees were, from the beginning, frequently involved in disciplinary matters such as the dismissal of absentees created an adverse judgement of them, echoes of which remained alive until the recent campaign for the election of a new President for the Miners' Union. Arthur Scargill, the left-wing contender who, in 1981, won a large majority, published a number of articles in which he opposed "participatory" schemes on the grounds that consultation had confused the roles of trade union representatives.

Of course, many trade unionists would argue that joint consultation produced certain positive results, although there is some evidence that the main gains arose where trade unions were strong enough to ignore the constraints involved in the advisory role which was prescribed. Where trade unions began actually to bargain on material questions, the balance tilted to the workpeople. Thus workpeople tended to see their gains as resulting from their own organizational power, and where it did not, they responded with even more alienation to all those entreaties about "making consultation work". Not surprisingly, the system began to generate complaints.

Even before the unions pushed forward to criticise, socialist thinkers had begun to develop similar notions, and these were sometimes outspoken. Notable among such advocates was R.H. Tawney, who was later to be lionised as a patriarch of revisionism in the Labour Party, but whose last long article, which appeared in *Socialist Commentary* was insistently radical on this theme. The Labour Government, he wrote "increased freedom by enlarging the range of alternatives between which ordinary men can choose; but it did little to remove from wage earners the sense that they belong to a class treated as instruments for ends dictated from above". It was in this important statement that Tawney enjoined future Labour Governments, to "use the industries in public ownership as a laboratory", along the lines we discussed in Chapter 1. As we said then, these valedictory words were never to be taken seriously by Tawney's professed followers, although they were very much in the minds of the renewed workers' control movement which began to emerge in the middle 1960s.

*   *   *

Nationalisation received an increasingly bad press through the 1960s and in to the 1970s. A part of this was politically biased, based simply on Conservative prejudices. But part of it arose because even while the fundamental status of workers did not change under public ownership, organizational centralization provoked its own opposing ethos. It is interesting that the manifesto of Mr. Schumacher, *Small is Beautiful*, was composed by a Coal Board official. He had reason to know.

During the 1960s, furthermore, extensive rationalization schemes laid waste half the coal mines and a considerable proportion of the railway system which had been taken over. The labour force in these basic industries was swingeingly cut. Nationalisation in fact carried through purges on a scale which could not at all easily have been mounted even by modern multinational companies.

But throughout the majority of this period, the maintenance of

full employment appeared to justify Strachey's perception, that
crises being manageable, moderate reform was an adequate
political strategy. The Labour Government of 1964-70 began to
experience the effects of the collapse of this viewpoint, which had
previously been elaborated at book length by C.A.R. Crosland and
several other imitators. One Minister in that Government ruefully
explained how, in the context of the collapsing world order of
Keynesianism, all the economic levers of conventional management
now became unresponsive to control. "We trod on the brake, and
nothing stopped" he said, "or, we pushed the accelerator and
nothing went". It was in this dawning knowledge that the Labour
Party began the 1970s with an agenda leading towards very radical
change.

*   *   *

Stuart Holland, the main inspirer of current Labour Party
economic policy, cut his teeth on the problems we are discussing
when he served in the Prime Minister's Office during Mr. Wilson's
early term. It was while he was observing the political process from
this central station that he developed his concept of the "meso-
economic" sector, of multinational companies, suspended between
the macro and micro sectors, but powerful enough to negate macro
decisions at the state level. The problem which Government faced
in dealing with multinational companies was that it lacked certain
basic expertise, which could only be developed by official agencies
if they were able to act in concert with trade unions. This novel
concept of a partnership between Government and trade unions in
pursuit of control over planning and investment policies came to
dominate Labour Party thinking, even though this was very
imperfectly reflected in the press and communications media.

Thus Labour Party policy on the democratic control of industry
offers proposals which, if they were ever implemented, would mark
a radical new departure in Britain. The notion of planning
agreements was conceived as central to this:

"The key to our planning effort is the domination of the economy by a
few leading firms. For by concentrating our major firms in
manufacturing — and especially the 100 or so major firms in
manufacturing — we can ensure that our planning is kept both
manageable and straightforward. We will harness directly the energies
of these giants — leaving the numerous smaller firms to our more

general planning policies. Two points of principle, however, we must make clear.

First, that in seeking to operate directly upon the activities of these leading firms, we are interested not so much in the day-to-day or month-to-month *tactics* which they will need to employ — how much they should produce, say, of each particular product — but in their medium and longer term *strategies*. That is, we are concerned to influence and shape their strategic programmes on investment, on location, on training, on import substitution and the like.

Second, that we will not attempt to meet precisely a set of over-detailed economic targets or expect to bring about a miraculous spurt in economic growth. Certainly, we do intend to make a major forecasting effort, and to establish — in consultation with both sides of industry — clear and identifiable targets. But our *prime* aim will be to achieve certain very broad objectives in terms of jobs in certain regions, for example, in investment, or in exports. It is the fulfilment of these objectives, indeed, which is crucial to our whole economic strategy."[12]

A far-reaching scheme for monitoring this process was set forth in a seven-point programme which was offered to the electorate in the mid-'seventies:

"To get up-to-date information, on a systematic and continuing basis, from all companies within the system. This information will concern both past performance and *advance* programmes — programmes which can be checked at a later date, against results. And it will cover such areas as investment, prices, product development, marketing, exports and import requirements.

To use this information to help the Labour Government to identify and achieve its planning objectives and to plan for the redistribution of resource which will be needed to meet these objectives.

To get the agreement of the firms within the system — the written Planning Agreement — that they will help the Government to meet certain clearly defined objectives (e.g. a certain number of new jobs in a Development Area) — whilst leaving the *tactics* which will be needed to achieve these objectives to the companies themselves.

To provide for the regular revision of those arrangements, in the light of experience and progress.

To provide a systematic basis for making large companies accountable for their behaviour, and for bringing into line those which refuse to co-operate — using, where necessary, both the extensive powers under our proposed Industry Act, the activities of our new and existing public enterprises, and the powers of public purchasing.

To publish and publicise a detailed annual report to the nation on the record of the companies within the system, and on the progress — or lack of it — towards meeting the nation's economic objectives."[13]

It was insisted that trade unions "must have the right to take part" both in drawing up the plans which were to be presented to the Government, and in the consultations about the final agreements. Later plans were announced to involve the 30 most important companies in such agreements by December 1976, and to comprehend the top 100 by the end of 1978. Twelve items for discussion were listed in the White Paper *The Regeneration of British Industry*:

1. Economic prospects
2. The Company's broad strategy and long term objectives
3. UK sales (sales for each main product line and the Company's market share)
4. Exports
5. Investment
6. Employment and Training
7. Productivity
8. Finance
9. Prices policy
10. Industrial Relations and arrangements for negotiation and consultation
11. Interests of consumers and community
12. Product and process development.[14]

The last five of these items being more complex than the first seven, it was suggested that they might not be tabled for consideration until 1976.

In fact, nothing at all happened, because in the cold coup d'etat which Mr. Wilson carried through in 1975, after the EEC referendum, planning agreements were made "voluntary" instead of compulsory. Hence, by February 1978 only one such agreement had been concluded, and that by Chrysler at the moment of their bankruptcy and receipt of Governmental doles. This was a purely token document. The annual report upon the new policy had nothing to say, and therefore did not appear.

The most crucial failure of planning agreements concerned the Lucas Aerospace corporate plan, which has become famous all over our continent. Fearing large scale redundancies as a result of cuts in military expenditure, the Shop Stewards' Combine Committee representing the numerous plants of Lucas Aerospace lobbied Mr. Tony Benn at the Department of Industry for help. He asked them to work out their own alternative proposals, which they immediately began to do. Unfortunately, Benn was subsequently dismissed, before the Lucas workers were able to prepare their monumental report in which more than a thousand pages of plans for socially useful products including many new inventions, were distilled from extensive enquiries throughout the industry. A great deal has been written about this extraordinary project, but it is a very sad commentary upon the Labour Government of 1974-79 that it failed to do anything to bring the Lucas plan within the framework of its proposed planning agreements. However, the idea of planning agreements continues to develop, and similar proposals now feature in the programmes of many Socialist Parties, from Greece through to Portugal.

Whilst the concept of planning agreements will clearly continue to demand attention, the Lucas proposals, and the proposals of the growing number of imitators of the Aerospace workers, raise new issues for democratic planning which have moved far outside the parameters accepted by the Webbs and Strachey. Originally conceived as a means of exerting social control over otherwise capricious multinational power, the planning agreements strategy has provoked workers to think of something hitherto rarely conceivable: the democratisation of the entrepreneurial function. Now, in the absence of Government support, local councils and other democratic bodies anxiously consult with the Lucas shop stewards about how job creation schemes involving the proposed new products might be launched by co-operative or municipal agencies. All this opens up the need for a whole variety of new democratic agencies: servicing bodies, trade mechanisms, advisory organizations, training schemes designed to facilitate such initiatives. This kind of thinking is still, in 1982, in its earliest stages, but we may be sure that the debate already in progress will produce a rich crop of new ideas.

*   *   *

It is difficult to predict how far the growth in co-operative and municipal enterprise will be able to develop. But however small this growth may be, it is likely to exercise a powerful influence on the reorganization of nationalised industries, and on the constitutions of the industries which are taken into public ownership in the future.

Already in the 1960s, workpeople were expressing strong dissatisfaction with the Morrisonian public utility as an organizational form. In 1967, under the influence of the workers' control movement, the National Craftsmen's Co-ordinating Committee of the Iron and Steel industry worked out a full-fledged programme for the re-entry of their industry into the public sector.

The nationalization measure which was actually brought in, was a repeat of those of the late 1940s, except that a token force of 'worker-directors', without specific powers or accountability, was built in at the last moment. These were appointed by management, as one of them subsequently described:

> "One morning, our general manager sent for me and said, 'Oh, the managing director wants to see you'. 'What the hell for?', I said, 'I haven't done any bloody thing!' "[15]

Twelve such persons, chosen from a list submitted by the TUC without the intervention of any of their workmates, and sworn to preserve the confidentiality of whatever boardroom secrets they might inadvertently uncover, soon came to the opinion 'we're accountable to BSC . . . we're not representatives of the unions at all'.

Setbacks in steel did not prevent others from pressing for greater powers, however. After the work-in at Upper Clyde Shipbuilders, when the demand for nationalisation of the shipbuilding industry was accepted by the Labour Party, a group of workers in the industry at Barrow met with their Member of Parliament, Albert Booth, to discuss plans for a management structure for public ownership. They, too, reached agreement on parity representation on the predominant policy-making board.

But in the aircraft industry, also scheduled for nationalization by the 1974 Labour administrators, workers raised their sights. Half a year before the return of Mr. Wilson to Downing Street, the Bristol workers of the British Aircraft Corporation published a thorough and detailed plan for the administration of their industry by a controlling council of worker representatives, elected by trade unionists, which would hire and fire management. "We reject worker-directors," they wrote: "the essence of our system is that management is hired by the workers to run the industry."

> "If the TUC means that 50 per cent trade union representation shall be directly elected via the trade union machinery in the nationalised industry so as to represent the workers employed in the industry then to that extent it is a movement towards the objectives we have raised earlier. We now come however to our fundamental and basic objection: What we would ask is the significance of the 50 per cent representation? The question surely is, does this or does it not give control? If not, it does not matter much whether the representation is 5 per cent, 10 per cent or 50 per cent. On the other hand if it is supposed that the proposed representation could mean the exercise of effective control over decision-making (albeit in certain areas) what are the arguments against a complete break with considerations about what different numerical

representations might mean and give overall control to elected worker representatives? The Report would seem to suggest that the trade unionists on a public board can represent workers, help to arrive at decisions and presumably as individuals make an equal contribution as any one of the other 50 per cent nominees, but that they could not be 'trusted' to make the 'right' decisions on their own. This is a strange reflection when considered in terms of local authorities up and down the country where elected councillors are responsible for the expenditure of considerable public funds and important policy decisions. It might be argued that local authorities have to work within central government's legislative and other constraints but to a lesser or greater extent this is true of the Public Sector in general and would certainly be so as far as a publicly owned aircraft industry was concerned. We cannot therefore understand why both the TUC documents fail even to discuss the proposition that the overall policy-making body of a publicly owned industry could be composed entirely of directly elected trade unionists who work in the industry concerned and that they should be clearly answerable and responsible to those who elected them.''[16]

Similar attitudes were expressed by the dockworkers of Hull and London, when the prepared their plan for the nationalisation of the Ports. In every other part of the public sector, these views find their echoes, sometimes stronger, sometimes more muted, sometimes intimidated by adversities and closures, but always present and never completely stifled.

The Thatcher administration has been energetically diminishing the public sector in Britain, by systematically selling off its more profitable assets.[17] At the same time, private bankruptcies have reached hitherto unimaginable levels. A future Labour Government would enter office with the commitment to renationalize all the hived-off assets of existing public industries, and also with the expectation that public intervention would head off industrial collapse in the private sector, far more aggressively than hitherto.

Throughout the slump, trade unions have become industrially quiescent for understandable reasons. It seems unlikely that their political attitudes will have been similarly restricted by adversity. In all probability, the demand for democratisation of Britain's nationalised and re-nationalised industries will re-emerge as a major political issue if the Labour Party returns to office during this decade.

Footnotes

1. John Strachey: *The Nature of Capitalist Crisis*, Gollancz, p.342.
2. Herbert Morrison: *Socialisation and Transport*, Constable, 1933.

3. Labour Party: *Annual Conference Report*, 1946.
4. *The Times*, 28 October 1946, p.2.
5. *Hansard*, HC Debs 418 5s 29 January 1946 C769-70.
6. Emmanuel Shinwell: *Conflict Without Malice*, Odhams, 1955, pp.172-3.
7. The Communist Party: *The Miners' Next Step*, September 1948, pp.13-16.
8. P.S. Bagwell: *The Railwaymen*, Allen and Unwin, London, 1963, p.623.
9. *Ibid.*
10. *Workers' Control?* Fabian Society, Tract No.271, 1951, p.67.
11. *Universities and Left Review*, No.3, Winter 1958, pp.59-60.
12. *Labour's Programme*, 1973.
13. *Ibid.*, p.18.
14. HMSO: *The Regeneration of British Industry*, August 1974.
15. P. Brannen, E. Batstone, D. Fatchett and P. White: *The Worker Directors*, Hutchinson, 1976, p.120.
16. Bristol Aircraft Workers: *A New Approach to Public Ownership*, IWC pamphlet No.43, 1974, pp.10-11.
17. Cf. Sue Hastings and Hugo Levie: *Privatisation?*, Spokesman 1983.

CHAPTER SEVEN

Castrating Bullock

The years of the Heath administration provoked a great radicalization of the trade unions. First, the Industrial Relations Act of 1971 brought them on to the streets, to begin with in vast official demonstrations, and later in a spontaneous outburst of collective rage, when the first victims of the Act made their way into prison. Second, the policy of allowing industrial "lame ducks" to die off provoked the work-in of Upper Clyde Shipbuilders in 1971, and this triggered an unprecedented movement of work-ins, sit-ins and general strike actions in defence of jobs, all of which had the direct effect of making an issue of the rights of workers to be involved in strategic decision-making, and some of which directly posed the question of workers' control. Third, successive conflicts over pay policies provoked more and more fraught conflicts, involving millions of people, and culminating in an enforced three-day week, followed by a miners' strike and a General Election in which the Government finally fell.

Seldom has the British Establishment lost its nerve so completely as during those days. When Mr. Wilson re-formed a minority Labour administration, there was little it could not have done, had it only had the will. The fact that the Conservatives had deliberately set out to curb the powers of the trade union interest, and over-ridden all opposition, was a clear and open invitation to Labour to respond by rolling back precisely those irresponsible powers of capital against which various Labour leaders had fulminated on successions of mayday celebrations and miners' gala festivals. This, however, was not Mr. Wilson's intention: the Establishment having come adrift from its moorings, his one over-riding instinct was to navigate it back into place again.

With a little help from his friends, this is precisely what he did.

Whatever happened to Industrial Democracy?

A few months before the fall of Mr. Heath, on the morning of Tuesday, October 2nd 1973, Ken Fleet, who was delegated by his (Beeston) Labour Party, but who is better-known as the secretary of the Institute for Workers' Control, went to the rostrum at the Party's Annual Conference in Blackpool, to move a composite resolution on Industrial Democracy. After a debate in which a number of leading spokesmen participated, including Eric Heffer, Roy Jenkins, Michael Meacher and others, his motion was approved so overwhelmingly that no-one called for a card vote.

The motion began with what at the time was almost a ritual salute to Tony Benn's celebrated watchword, committing the Party to "a fundamental and irreversible shift in the balance of wealth and power, in favour of working people and their families". It went on to spell out a quite specific range of measures:

"Conference welcomes the determination to extend public ownership and control, especially in the key growth sectors of the economy, but is convinced that for this policy to be carried through successfully, to win widespread support and to become the basis for fundamental changes in the social structure, strong and genuine elements of industrial democracy and workers' control will have to be introduced in all nationalised industries. It is essential that structures be imposed which will allow for the full exercise of the talents and democratic rights of the workers in those companies, that these include the direct election of trades unionists at all levels under arrangements agreed with and supervised by the trades unions concerned; the Board of each nationalised industry must be composed of at least 50 per cent trades unionists elected in this way, and workers must have the right of veto over all executive appointments including that of the chairman. Workers' representatives must have equal rights and powers with other members of these boards and complete access to all information concerning their industries and enterprises and be required to report back fully to their constituents and be subject to recall by these constituents."

The intervention of Roy Jenkins in this discussion was a remarkably nervous and cautious one. He spoke with a considerable passion, to insist that

"We need to promise no more than we are convinced we can do".

At the same time, Roy Jenkins gave the studied impression that he had no objection to the extension of democracy into public sector industries:

"It is not good taking over a vast number of industries without a clear plan as to how and by whom they are to be run. It is no good pretending a transfer of ownership in itself solves our problems."

In reply to this and other interventions, Tony Benn, speaking for the Executive, went out of his way to widen the argument: accepting that "nationalisation plus Lord Robens does not add up to socialism", he called for a bold response: "industrial democracy begins now", he said . . . "if we are only concerned to win the votes we shall never mobilize the strength we need to implement the policy . . . if we win the argument we shall win the election". "We are offering much more than legislation," he went on: "we are offering a perspective and a vision which will transform the political atmosphere of cynicism which has developed in recent years. Without a vision people will turn to their immediate and narrow self-interests. With some sense that they are part of a change in our society we shall be able to draw much more from them . . ." If this was a response to Mr. Jenkins' previous plea not to "add to the dangerous public disillusionment with parties, with politics and with politicians", Tony Benn's next remark was directed at future adversaries rather than past ones:

"One delegate said that we shall inherit a crisis when we come to power. We are saying . . . that the crisis that we inherit when we come to power will be the occasion for fundamental change and not the excuse for postponing it."

It was with these words in their minds that Labour activists went into the two election campaigns of 1974.

The October 1974 Election manifesto contained an explicit pledge to honour the decisions previously reached in this and other Labour Party Conferences. 'We will,' it said, 'introduce new legislation to help forward our plans for a radical extension of industrial democracy in both the private and public sectors. This will involve major changes in company law and in the statutes which govern the nationalised industries and the public services.' Already in February 1974, the previous Manifesto had pledged 'We intend to socialise the nationalised industries. In consultation with the unions, we shall take steps to make the management of existing nationalised industries more responsible to the workers in the industry and more responsive to their consumers' needs.'

For a brief while it appeared as though Tony Benn's formula for meeting "the crisis that we shall inherit" was capable of application. With the repeal of the Industrial Relations Act of 1971, the tabling of the Employment Protection Act, and a variety of other measures, the defensive needs of the Trades Union Congres were swiftly met, at any rate in substantial measure. Hopes of democratic innovation were held out by the funding (albeit inadequately) of three worker co-operatives in collapsing private sector enterprises: at Meriden, Triumph Motorcycles; at Kirkby, KME, manufacturing radiators and a range of other products; and the Scottish Daily News in Glasgow. Bitter fights between ministers (and above all, the Secretary of State for Industry, Tony Benn himself) and senior civil servants became daily rituals during these days.

Then, with the defeat of the Labour Party, at the hands of a coalition embracing most of its own Government and virtually the entire political and media Establishments, in the Referendum on membership of the European Economic Community, came the counter-revolution. Tony Benn was instantly dismissed from his department, and given Energy instead. Various others were removed. Eric Heffer had already been pushed out before the Referendum had taken place. The Industry Act was then instantly filleted by Prime Ministerial command. New co-operatives were nipped in the bud by allowing the work-ins at Imperial Typewriters in Hull and Norton Villiers Triumph to sink unaided, and by installing Eric Varley at the Department of Industry. (Mr. Varley, who as a mineworker had been an effective partisan of workers' control, has shown a remarkable political consistency. When he became a Member of Parliament, he favoured Parliamentary control, and once he was minister, he was immediately converted to ministerial control. The unifying principle, as may be readily seen, is the appealingly simple one of Varley's control. Happily, this is a Platonic ideal. Whilst showing great virtuosity in the pursuit of office Mr. Varley seems to have no particular ideas about how to employ it once obtained.)

Having thus met the threat of fundamental change head-on, Harold Wilson then set about postponing it indefinitely. In August 1975 Peter Shore announced the intention to appoint a committee of enquiry on whether or not the Election manifestos were to be carried out:

> "Accepting the need for a radical extension of industrial democracy in the control of companies by means of representation on boards of directors, and accepting the essential role of trade union organisations in this process, to consider how such an extension can best be achieved, taking into account in particular the proposals of the Trades Union Congress report on industrial democracy as well as experience in Britain, the EEC and other countries. Having regard to the interest of the national economy,

employees, investors and consumers, to analyse the implications of such representation for the efficient management of companies and for company law."

It took until December to find an appropriate mix of experts to staff this committee: and then after that it took until January 1977 for the subsequent *Report* to be agreed and published. The policy of the TUC, following upon the circulation, during Mr. Heath's administration, of the EEC's fifth directive, (which proposed a modified form of co-determination on the lines of German company law, as a possible European standard) had been to press for a 50% share of company direction. Lord Bullock's Committee, which included three representatives of the TUC (Jack Jones, Clive Jenkins and David Lea) also involved three company chairmen (Norman Biggs of Williams and Glyn's bank; Sir Jack Callard of ICI; Mr. Barrie Heath of Guest, Keen and Nettlefolds Ltd.) and a sprinkling of lawyers and academics, one of whom (John Methven) was to leave the newly appointed Committee in order to become director of the Confederation of British Industry. It was perfectly clear that this mix had been designed in order to encourage a watering down of the TUC's inconvenient ideas. This was duly accomplished, although to a lesser extent than was probably intended. The Committee recommended in favour of parity control of the larger companies only, but with an intervening group of mutually acceptable "independents" holding the balance. This was the "$2x + y$" formula, which, accompanied by a great deal of small print, helped to secure a certain loss of interest among the shop stewards whose active pressure alone could ensure the success of the scheme. The most effective and carefully worked out part of the Report concerned the problem of co-ordinating workpeople's trade union representation within firms, but, sage though this was (reflecting the draftsmenship of Jack Jones himself and Bill Wedderburn?) it was generally overlooked in the dispute which then broke out between the major unions. The Engineers (AUEW), normally fiercely divided between left and right factions, showed a united front against the proposals. They were followed by the electricians (EETPTU), and, at a discreet and less intransigent distance, by the General and Municipal Workers. It was no small feat of management on the part of Jack Jones that he held the TUC consensus through all such divisions. The 1977 Congress approved a resolution in these terms:

"This Congress welcomes the analysis of the Bullock Committee Report highlighting the need for industrial democracy and reaffirms its belief in legislative action in this field. This does not assume that the only way forward is to legislate for worker representation on the policy-making boards of companies. This Congress is convinced that collective bargaining can be extended to greatly increase trade union influence over main policies. The extension of worker representation on policy boards or committees should not be used as a means of frustrating the processes of existing collective bargaining machinery. Congress calls upon the Government to legislate for full disclosure of information necessary to enable trade union representatives to properly represent their members.

In order to maintain maximum unity within the trade union Movement on this issue, Congress calls upon the General Council to press the Labour Government to provide for statutory backing to all unions wishing to establish joint control of strategic planning decisions via trade union machinery. This legislation would include the option of parity representation on the board, but would also link up with more flexible forms of joint regulation more clearly based on collective bargaining. Congress further believes that the objective of making the public sector of industry serve social purposes will be strengthened by effective worker participation on management boards and urges immediate steps to implement the proposals of the Nationalised Industries Committee for parity trade union representation on the boards of nationalised industries where it is the wish of the members."

By now it was September

Mr. Edmund Dell, now Secretary for Trade, had promised legislation "during the 1977 session". It was clear that time was running short.

At the beginning of the following month, the Labour Party Conference approved a somewhat stronger resolution, from the Iron and Steel Trades Confederation, about the lack of progress in the Nationalised industries. This viewed

"with concern the apparent lack of progress towards democracy in industry."

It went on to urge "the Government as an act of faith in Socialist principle to speedily implement the movement towards industrial democracy in the nationalised industries. Nevertheless Conference believes that participation must extend from the shop floor to the main board, be permitted to be flexible, allowing for the history of industrial relations in the industry concerned, and firmly based on the trade union machinery as an adjunct to traditional collective bargaining."

Something had been done about this in the Post Office, where a participatory top-level structure had been agreed: and active consultations did go ahead with the mineworkers. But in general, very little actually happened. This did not stop the circulation of minutes, however.

It was not until May 1978 that the discussions within the small circle of secretaries of state (Education, Employment, Trade: under the chairmanship of Shirley Williams, wearing her hat as Paymaster General) had reached the point where a white paper might be offered up. This wondered whether various things might be done: a code of practice might be drawn up by an Industrial Democracy Commission "if one is set up". Failing this, ACAS "might be invited to draw it up with a view to its being submitted to Parliament for approval". The one solid bone offered to the unions was that the Joint Representation Committees recommended by Bullock might be established, not to implement any prescribed reform, but in order to discuss company strategy. From a fundamental and irreversible shift in the balance of wealth and power, the circle had moved to show

> "the object of participation is understanding and co-operation . . . recourse to statutory fall-back arrangements will be the exception."

Board representation, but not on terms of parity, was to become a statutory right after an interim of "three to four years from the date of establishment of the Joint Representation Committee".

Even this limited object remained an aspiration. No legislative proposals were ever made, either in May 1978 or thereafter.

Not surprisingly, the General Council did not mark this tepid document very high. Gamma-minus was about all it rated. They "considered that the Government were proposing a very protracted timetable for the attainment of . . . modest objectives".

The Prime Minister greeted the white paper with a hope that legislation might be tabled in the 1978-9 session. This would have brought the matter round to the mid-'eighties before any notion of compulsion came into play. In November 1978 the Queen's Speech to a Parliament which was doomed to dissolution promised to legislate

> "to ensure that employees and unions were able to participate in discussions of corporate strategy, and to provide in due course for employee representation on company boards."

By April 1979 this had still not materialized.

At the beginning of this long process, the TUC had been calling for parity involvement in company boards, by which it meant 50% representation for workplace union representatives. By the time

Bullock reported, the $2X + y$ formula had diluted the notion of parity, and the main union advance proposed was the establishment of effective JRCs, which could solve the problem of representation at combine level. In the white paper, the German system originally rejected by the TUC had now re-emerged, but with minor adjustments towards the employers' interests. Parity had already become a "phased" target: it was difficult to see why any self-respecting shop steward should wish to embroil himself in such a stew of compromise and equivocation. Rank-and-file enthusiasm, diminished by each successive devaluation of the original project, was already moving towards zero quite some time before the Queen pronounced a promise of legislation that was never to come.

The strategy of company law reform, properly considered, may still have something to commend it to socialists: but it is doubtful whether the Bullock Report will ever be debated again. A much more apposite reform was proposed during 1971, at the time of the UCS work-in, by Tony Benn. It would simply have required, as an annual ritual upon which continued registration as a limited company would depend, the depositing of a certificate of acceptability signed by the relevant workpeople's representatives. This would enable the unions to negotiate whatever degree and style of participatory involvement seemed appropriate to them.

CHAPTER EIGHT

Lords and Quangos

There is probably no better indicator of the lapse into conformity and mind-numbing conservatism which has been the inevitable expression of Labour's evolution under 'social-democratic' hegemony than the (at first sight) subordinate issue of the House of Lords.

For the popular press, and for some of the Labour front bench, this has become the badge of the 'bolshevism' of Tony Benn and his colleagues. Labour Party policy on this matter is transparently clear. This was the text of the motion moved by Jack Jones at the 1977 Conference:

"This Conference declares that the House of Lords is a negation of democracy and calls upon the Government, the Parliamentary Party and the National Executive Committee to take every possible step open to them to secure the total abolition of the House of Lords, and the reform of Parliament into an efficient, single chamber, legislating body, without delay.

Conference calls for this measure to be included in the next manifesto as set out in the National Executive Committee paper. Conference instructs the National Executive Committee to organise a great campaign throughout the movement on this issue."[1]

Never has a resolution been more overwhelmingly adopted: 6,248,000 votes were recorded in its favour, to 91,000 against.

The reasoned case for this commitment was argued in a statement submitted by the National Executive Committee to the same Conference:

"Since the publication of our 1976 Programme, the House of Lords has shown by its actions that our description of it is more than justified — and the Lords have shown quite clearly that action to deal with an unrepresentative Second Chamber can no longer be delayed.

The main function of the Lords is supposed to be that of a revising chamber but, as the Prime Minister has pointed out, it has taken on the role of a wrecking chamber. Most of the major pieces of legislation of the 1975/76

Session: the Aircraft and Shipbuilding Industries Bill, the Rent (Agriculture) Bill, the Education Bill, the Dockwork Regulation Bill, and the Health Services Bill — were emasculated in the Lords on Committee Stage and Third reading, so that they emerged virtually unrecognisable.

While admittedly some of the amendments were just tidying-up amendments, others were very substantial indeed. For example, on the Aircraft and Shipbuilding Bill, the *Sunday Times* reported on 7th November 1976 that the Lords amendments would:

'delete all ship-repairing, prohibit British shipbuilders from operating any ships, and delay vesting day of the aircraft industry until after the next General Election.'

The House of Lords with its inbuilt Conservative majority, has always been hostile to Labour Governments, but even so the Lords are now being far more destructive than they were in the 1960s. In the period of the last Labour Government, between 1964 and 1970, the number of divisions in the Lords averaged 40 per year. However, in the 1974-75 session the Government was *defeated* in 100 Lords divisions and in the recent 1975-76 session it was *defeated* in 120 divisions. It suffered eight defeats on the Rent (Agricultural) Bill, 11 on the Education Bill, 11 on the Race Relations Bill, 17 on the Health Services Bill, 25 on the Aircraft and Shipbuilding Bill and 28 on the Dockwork and Regulation Bill.

The fifth Marquess of Salisbury, who was a noted right-winger, has been quoted as saying with reference to the 1945-51 Labour Government:

'The Conservative Peers came to the conclusion that where something was in the Labour Party manifesto we would regard it as approved by the country . . .'

Yet now the Conservatives in the Lords appear not even to accept that. In two election Manifestoes in 1974 Labour stated clearly that 'we shall (also) take (ports), shipbuilding, ship-repairing and marine engineering, and the aircraft industries into public ownership and control'. However, the Lords insisted on deleting ship-repairing from the Bill, despite the fact that the Bill had already had approximately 200 hours of Commons time, and that the Lords amendments had been rejected by the elected House of Commons several times.

Apparently, two general election victories are not enough to satisfy the House of Lords. They would it seems, prefer to rely on the considered judgement of such members of the Upper House as Viscount Simon:

'I find it difficult to believe that this suggestion for nationalisation started at the work bench. Naturally, I have no evidence and I am only expressing a view in the light of the way people think, but I cannot believe that the average workman thinks about that sort of thing at all.'

Of course, as has been said before, the House of Lords only takes on this role of 'interpreter of the People's minds' when Labour Governments are in office as opposed to the Conservatives. It is instructive to contrast the action of the House of Lords at present with their action (or lack thereof) on the EEC Bill when the last Conservative Government was in office:

'The Bill was brief and incomplete... in their anxiety to pass the Bill into law, the Government had allowed no time for Amendments, even on a drafting point.'[2]

The Conservative majority in the House of Lords duly ensured that this major piece of legislation went through unamended, without so much as a dot or comma changed, and proceeded to pass it by a majority of 393.

It is clear that, as the Prime Minister said in the House of Commons,

'. . . time after time after time there has been a conspiracy between the Conservative front bench in this House and the inbuilt Conservative majority in the House of Lords to defeat legislation which has been passed through this House.'[3]

The Guardian pointed out on 27th October 1976 that the Government had up to then been defeated in 48 out of 49 divisions, and concluded that:

'By far the heaviest weight behind the votes on these 48 occasions, both in the moving of the amendments, and the manning of the divisions lobbies, has come from the Conservative peers and those Independents who invariably support them. What is more, the insurmountable advantage which the Conservatives get from their army of hereditary members has been the main determining factor in the major votes. Four out of five of those who voted to cut the dockwork zone, four out of five who wrote the delaying power into the aircraft and shipbuilding Bills, were hereditary peers — only very few of them peers of first creation. The main reason why the Government has sustained such a string of defeats in the Lords is that the Conservatives have been able to use their superior power in the unelected Upper house to do what they do not have the strength to do in the elected Lower.'

This is clearly a situation which the Labour Party cannot allow to continue."[4]

This, then, was the imperative which was specifically disobeyed by Mr Callaghan, who went to the point of exerting a personal veto (to which it is arguable, he was not entitled) over writing any such commitment into the 1979 election manifesto.

Now, how would the ethical social democrats have viewed this matter before the great apostasy? Let us listen to Tawney:

> "Talk is nauseous without practice. Who will believe that the Labour Party means business as long as some of its stalwarts sit up and beg for social sugar-plums, like poodles in a drawing-room... And, if Privy Councillors make up for the part, when duty requires it, by hiring official clothes from a theatrical costume-maker, who will let them for the day at not unreasonable rates, that is nothing to shed tears over, except their discomfort. The thing, all the same, though a trifle, is insincere, and undignified. Livery and an independent mind go ill together. Labour has no need to imitate an etiquette. It can make its own . . .
>
> To kick over an idol, you must first get off your knees. To say that snobbery is inevitable in the Labour Party, because all Englishmen are snobs, is to throw up the sponge. Either the Labour Party means to end the tyranny of money, or it does not. If it does, it must not fawn on the owners and symbols of money. If there are members of it— a small minority no doubt, but one would be too many — who angle for notice in the capitalist Press; accept, or even beg for, 'honours'; are flattered by invitations from fashionable hostesses; suppose that their financial betters are endowed with intellects more dazzling and characters more sublime than those of common men; and succumb to convivial sociabilities, like Red Indians to fire-water, they have mistaken their vocation. They would be happier as footmen. It may be answered, of course, that it is sufficient to leave them to the ridicule of the world which they are so anxious to enter, and which may be trusted in time— its favourites change pretty quickly — to let them know what it thinks of them. But in the meantime, there are such places as colliery villages and cotton towns. How can followers be Ironsides if leaders are flunkies?
>
> One cannot legislate for sycophancy; one can only expose it, and hope that one's acquaintances will expose it in oneself. The silly business of 'honours' is a different story. For Labour knighthoods and the rest of it (except when, as in the case of civil servants and municipal officers, such as mayors and town clerks, they are recognised steps in an official career) there is no excuse. Cruel boys tie tin cans to the tails of dogs; but even a mad dog does not tie a can to its own tail. Why on earth should a Labour member? He has already all the honour a man wants in the respect of his own people."[5]

Of course, in Tawney's day, patronage was the merest glint in the Prime Minister's eye. All the impassioned fireworks in this short passage were provoked by the conferment of two long-forgotten Knighthoods on Labour and Trade Union functionaries. Since then, not merely Knighthoods, but peerages themselves, have become ten-a-penny. Tawneys, unfortunately, among our social-democratic leaders, are incomparably rarer. Indeed Tawney sounds, does he not, uncommonly like a less reticent and more strident incarnation of Tony Benn? Benn, however, is a bolshevik, Tawney is dead, and how can moderate men run the country if there is no trough at which to dip the snouts of all who merit reward and recognition?

There were 129 union-sponsored M.P.s in October 1974. It would be laborious to calculate how many retired trade union leaders were, at that time, sitting in the other house: but by 1979 some fairly unlikely candidates had wound up on the list of life peers, which included not only Hugh Scanlon of the AUEW and Richard Briginshaw of NATSOPA, among other scourges of the Establishment, but also Lords Allen, Collison, Cooper, Williamson, Greene and Plant from the more conventional trade union centre. Mr. Wilson created 152 life peers between 1964 and 1970, and a further 79 (not counting those on his controversial resignation list, who came into Mr. Callaghan's roster) since February 1974. In all, 155 peers take the Labour whip, 28 of whom are hereditary peers, and the remainder, life peers. Mr. Wilson also named at least 360 Knights Bachelor between 1964 and 1970, and no less than 136 since early 1974. In two periods of office, he named 24 chairmen of nationalised industry boards. This vast mill of patronage is felt far further afield than in the trade union movement, and the social weight of an OBE is probably not what once it was. But Prime Ministerial consideration is only the summit of a mountainous apparatus of other forms of official perferment, which at its lower levels may seem to be more socially functional, and therefore in some senses more justifiable than it appears to many trade unionists when it is plainly a matter of baubles and trinkets.

Before the second world war, the TUC General Council only nominated members to one dozen government appointed committees or statutory bodies. By 1948 TUC nominees were present on 60 such bodies. In origin all of these were seen as utilitarian institutions: but in practice many of them became sinecures, and were to be preferred to the purely honorific status of "Lord" this or "Sir" that because they commonly carried either a fee or a regular income, which was a valuable supplement to the retirement pension of an outgoing General Councillor.

Robert Taylor reports that Sir John Hare, the Minister of Agriculture during the '50s, actually complained to the TUC "about the lack of effort being put in by union nominees serving at that time on the marketing boards". "At this time" he cites George Woodcock as commenting:

> There was no reporting back. We never knew what they were doing. In fact, they did damn all . . . [6]

Taylor goes on to report that when Vincent Tewson, an earlier TUC General Secretary, served on the (now defunct) National Economic Planning Board for the TUC "he did not even tell Woodcock what was happening".

Such Quangos (in American: Quasi-autonomous Non-Governmental Organizations; in English *National* Governmental) have become more and more common, and it would not be possible for a serious representative to sleep through the sessions of at any rate the more important ones.

Nonetheless, such bodies are often less effective than they might be, because they depend largely upon patronage for their existence, and lack either the legal powers or the democratic clout to compel attention. When the Health and Safety Executive goes to work, it does dispose of certain clearly defined powers which it applies within a clearly defined set of responsibilities. This is less true when we consider the work of such bodies as the Equal Opportunities Commission, or the Commission for Racial Equality, both of which concern issues of much importance.

Ideally, representative forms of democratic alliance could be evolved to discharge such functions of these bodies as are necessary, in the context of as much legislative support as might be needed. As things are, members of such quangos do not have much muscle, mainly *because* they remain unaccountable to their wider constituencies.

The incredible growth of State patronage with the growth of the State itself raises vast problems for the Labour movement. The answer of socialists will, it is unnecessary to say, not follow the prescription of the Thatcher Government, which is to amputate any useful organ of Government that seems to move. On the contrary, quangos commonly represent feeble concessions to vast areas of need which positively demand not less, but more, effective social intervention. Precisely for this reason, the machinery for such intervention should be constituted as democratically as possible, and rendered as accountable as is practicable to the relevant constituencies. Otherwise the numerous matters of public policy involved will all suffer from having their spokesmen stitched into the fabric of a fundamentally unrepresentative and elitist establishment.

All this renders Tawney's simple prescription for patronage more difficult to apply: but that is no reason for forgetting:

If the only case for 'honours' is the practical one, it seems pretty easy to meet. Let the next party conference lay down (1) that no member of the party shall accept adornments of the kind except from a Labour government, (2) that no Labour government shall confer any 'honours' except such as are essential in order to enable it to do the job for which it was given power. Were that course adopted, a Labour government would remain free to recommend the creation of such peers and Privy Councillors as it required. But we should see less of the humiliating business of Labour members succumbing, however undesignedly, to the blandishments of a social system which the Labour Party is pledged to do its utmost to wind up.[7]

Status is one thing. Structural unemployment is another. But the attitudes of those on the right who are leaving the Labour party show a complete lack of appreciation of the morality of the great social democrats, whether in defending full employment as the priority of all priorities, or in approaching equality. Tawney's passionate calls for an end to flummery and obsequiousness were not simply objections to fancy dress and medieval badges: they were a heart-cry for the recognition of common humanity, which is always brought under attack when one man or woman is (however ritually) subordinated to another.

Footnotes
1. The Labour Party: *Report of 76th Annual Conference*, p.270.
2. Janet Morgan: *The House of Lords and the Labour Government*, 1967-70, p.233.
3. *Hansard* 9th November 1976, Col.211.
4. The Labour Party: *Statements to Annual Conference*, October 1977, pp.13-15.
5. R.H. Tawney: *The Attack and Other Papers*, Allen and Unwin, 1953, pp.66-68, Spokesman edition 1981.
6. Robert Taylor: *The Fifth Estate*, Routledge, 1978.
7. Letter to *New Statesman*, 22 June 1935, reproduced in issue of 11 June 1976.

CHAPTER NINE

Re-organising the Labour Party

Those leaving the Labour Party were also ostentatiously leaving behind their association with trade unions. There is apparently no room for such embarrassing organisations in the middle ground. For this reason it was easy for the social democrats to appeal to the principle of "one person, one vote" when settling their own constitution.

This principle is an important one to any democratic organisation, and we shall soon see it cause trouble in the new Alliance. But the Labour Party is a federation, with a conflicting plurality of more (or sometimes very much less) democratic affiliates, each defining its own rules of accountability and representation. Obviously it is not easy to rationalise such a structure, leave alone bring it to conformity with consistently democratic standards.

Nonetheless, central reforms are necessary and overdue, not to satisfy the defectors, but to assure the health and vitality of the federation itself, and to allow it to grow and develop.

*   *   *

The reform argument had been well under way before the 1979 defeat. The major dispute at the 1978 Labour Conference had concerned the defeat of the proposal for automatic reselection of Labour M.P.s, which would have ensured that a choice of candidates were interviewed by a selection conference once in the lifetime of every Parliament. This proposal would have ended the situation in which, once chosen, a Parliamentarian has had every expectation of survival right up to the moment of electoral defeat, or retirement, whichever has been the earlier. As it happened, as a result of a contentious vote, a compromise proposal was accepted, requiring sitting members to win a formal vote of confidence if they were to avoid appearing before a selection meeting. The argument about this issue was obviously not finally settled, and it was further developed during the next months in a variety of publications and meetings, after which the interim decision was changed.

However, an even more crucial issue was raised in the course of the 1978 ballot on this question. The reselection vote *would* have been won, had 877,000 votes of the Engineers' Union been cast in accordance with the repeated decision of the Union's Conference delegation. As things went, the mandatory reselection motion received 2,672,000 votes, and was opposed by 3,066,000. But the AUEW abstained. As *Tribune* reported:

> "As soon as the vote had been taken, the AUEW president, Hugh Scanlon, came to the rostrum to say that his delegation had abstained by mistake. They had intended, he said, to vote in favour of mandatory reselection and had they done so the outcome would have been reversed."[1]

Hugh Scanlon's version is, however, disputed by some AUEW delegates. They say that the delegation leader deliberately abstained, in defiance of the clearly expressed will of the delegation, at a meeting held only hours before. One AUEW delegate, Jock MacPherson Quinn, was also a conference teller. He says that when he offered the ballot box to Scanlon, Gavin Laird and John Boyd—who were sitting together—they replied that they weren't voting. When Quinn reminded them that they were mandated he was told to get on with his job as teller. By way of confirmation, a similar story had been featured in the *Guardian*:

> "One Union that might be angrily considering making its leader stand for re-election with the same regularity as some trade unions want Labour M.P.s to do, is the Amalgamated Union of Engineering Workers. When the votes were cast yesterday after the debate on reselection, there were some angry allegations that the outgoing president, Mr. Hugh Scanlon, had not carried out the mandated wishes of his members, coupled with some claims of high-handed and peremptory behaviour by the president-elect, Mr. Terry Duffy.
>
> Last Sunday all four sections of the AUEW met and voted to support an amendment concerning M.P.s reselection. But yesterday afternoon, just before the debate began, the union delegation was summoned to talk things over with its executive who had opposed the decision, and it was asked to reconsider. The delegates reconsidered—and decided by an even more decisive vote to stick to their original decision.
>
> At this, Mr. Duffy is reported to have got very angry, and a slanging match followed.
>
> When it came to the actual vote after the debate a teller, who happened to be from the AUEW, approached Mr. Scanlon so that he could cast the engineering section's vote. Mr. Scanlon said he was abstaining on this

amendment and waiting for another which had not yet been debated. The teller protested that this was not what the delegation wanted, and said he was told by Mr. Scanlon to 'go and do his job'.

It is being claimed that if the crucial 870,000 votes that Mr. Scanlon had in his hand had gone the way the union had decided it would have made all the difference to the final result."[2]

After enquiry, it is dificult to be certain about the reason for Hugh Scanlon's abstention, which some put down to confusion, whilst others still believe it to have been deliberate. Although, whatever might have been the cause, this was a sad event, there is no point in pursuing its motivation here. What is more important is the fact that the union executive was so concerned about this motion that it tried to secure a constitutional reversal of the delegation's decision to support it, and that a recalled delegation meeting was set up entirely for this purpose. This second meeting confirmed its original decision by 26 votes to 19, and when this happened,

"Duffy in the words of one observer 'went bananas'. He told them that they were overturning a unanimous decision of the union's executive (which is not true) and that nothing like this will happen in the future after he takes over."[3]

Of course, the Engineers' Union has a history of controversy upon this matter, and indeed, before the election of Hugh Scanlon to the Presidency, there was a long-running dog-fight on the matter of "Carron's Law".

This episode was summed up by David Edelstein and Malcolm Warner in their authoritative study on *Comparative Union Democracy*:

"It is one thing to make policy, but another to see that it is carried out . . . A . . . serious and more pervasive loss of the national committee's policy-making powers to the president took place under Lord Carron's right-wing rule, and ended only with Scanlon's election in 1967. It was made conspicuously evident by Carron casting the Engineers' massive block vote at conferences of the Trades Union Congress and the Labour Party in defiance of decisions of the national committee, under what became known as Carron's Law. However, a similar conflict between the national committee and executive council began in 1955, the year before that of Carron's election as president, over the question of support for the left-Labour Aneurin Bevan's bid for office in the Labour Party. The decision of the primarily rank-and-file delegation which was involved to the Labour Party conference was over-ruled by the executive council, which was represented in the conference delegation and claimed the power of decision in such matters. The Engineers' rules permit the executive council to appoint representatives from among its members and, together with the president and general secretary, to call a meeting of the delegation prior to the conference (Rule 44:1,2), but we see no grounds for the council claiming decision-making powers.

On the contrary, the rules state: 'All decisions of the National Committee shall be final and binding on the Executive Council' (Rule 14:8). Later in 1955, a decision of the rank-and-file appeals court supported the majority of the conference delegation, but the entire sequence was repeated in 1956 when a new national committee decision to support Bevan was again defied by the executive council at the Labour Party conference . . . Such defiance of the national committee, the Labour Party, TUC delegations and the appeals court was repeated under Carron's reign as president with differences only in detail:

'In 1965 the . . . National Committee carried a fervid motion pledging 100 per cent support for the Labour Government. What exactly constituted 100 per cent was not defined, but this difficulty did not embarrass Sir William. From now on, the AEU vote was forever to be stacked behind the Government . . . In the 1966 Labour Party Conference . . . 100 per cent was still no less. Sir William put aside all plaints from the delegates that the union had, in fact, gone on record against the American intervention in Vietnam, and in favour of cuts in military expenditure. From the moment that the Conference opened, he kept firm control of the pad upon which the votes of the delegation are recorded, and remorselessly plonked the AEU's 768,000 votes . . . straight down the line for the platform.' (Crisis of British Socialism, Spokesman 1972, pp.169-171)

The ridiculously mechanical nature of Carron's control at the conference is illustrated by what happened when he was called away on personal business; the pad for recording the delegation's block vote was passed to the most senior member, the left-Labour executive councillor Scanlon, who then proceeded to poll the delegation. The result was that the Labour Party conference did indeed pass resolutions for reducing military expenditure and against American intervention in Vietnam, with the support of the Engineers, a support which would have failed had Carron been present."[4]

These abuses of the union's votes at TUC as well as Labour Conferences resulted in a series of appeals to the Final Appeal Court of the Union.

"In a series of judgements in relation to Resolution 16 of the 1966 National Committee, it ruled against the Executive Committee's decision not to recall, and the failure to allow the TUC delegation its voting rights. In practice this was of as little immediate help to Carron's political opponents as had been the previous court decisions against him. As far as Carron was concerned the Final Appeal Court was stacked with his political opponents who were misusing the Constitution of the Union: if they were in his position they would be as against the Government as he was for it, and would use the union vote to disregard National Committee policy entirely. At this stage anyway, with only a year to retirement, he could afford to ignore the Court."[5]

Carron was twice censured by the Appeal Court, which was vested, constitutionally, with ultimate authority on the matters which came before it. As Minkin reports, this made no difference:

"At the Party Conference of 1967 Carron made his last stand with an effrontery which had one AEU delegate waving his crutch in rage. At the Saturday morning delegation meeting, he refused a discussion on the economic and incomes policies and then when delegates demanded a second meeting closed the meeting with a 'We'll see'. There was no second delegation meeting, and, on the floor of Conference, no pad was passed round the delegation despite yet another rowdy demonstration by members of the delegation."[6]

Norman Dinning has repudiated the suggestion that he "waved his crutch" but otherwise, this is a fair description of what happened. All the protests of AEU delegates achieved little indeed, until the Carron regime came to an end. Also in 1967, Sir William withheld the vote of the engineers from A. J. Forrester, who had been nominated for the National Executive Committee of the Party by DATA, the Draughtsmen's organization. The engineers' delegation had not only voted to give support to Forrester, but confirmed this decision when Hugh Scanlon queried the result at the delegation meeting. A recount took place, which underlined the delegation's support for Mr. Forrester. The vote, at that time numbering 768,000, was nonetheless withheld and Sir William never made any explanation as to why.

Is Carron's law to be restored, under a new name? If this is what Terry Duffy was threatening, the matter concerns not only members of his own organisation. 877,000 votes is more than the number in the hands of all the Constituency section of the Labour Party, taken together. If all the individual members of the Party are to have their wishes cancelled, by one functionary riding arbitrarily over the desires of his members, then there will arise a real political crisis which will have repercussions throughout the entire labour movement.

Various affiliated bodies have already requested the Labour Party Executive to give some sort of guidance on this question: and it would perhaps be useful if it were discussed at other levels, too.

Such considerations do not only apply to engineers. It was as a result of pressure from trade union leaders that an enquiry into the state of Party organization was established, as the *Guardian* reported:[7]

"Union leaders intent on holding a special Party Conference to discuss the results of the enquiry into Party organization, have set April as the target date for the meeting. If the Unions had their way, the Party would consist of the same delegates who got to the Brighton Conference. The main negotiations in the enquiry are being entrusted to a small group of Union leaders representing differing political attitudes in the Trade Unions."

In response to this, I wrote at the time:

"A question which is relevant is this: if a special Conference of the Labour Party takes place in April 1980, how many of the Trade Unions voting there will have held their Conferences before that date? On the assumption that some of the major unions will not in fact confer until after April, we can see that vast block votes may be cast on a number of crucial issues on which trade union leaders may never have consulted their members.

The reform of the Labour Party is a major issue, and many of us have pursued it for a long time. The few central issues which have been debated in Conference already have given union leaderships time to consult their members. But there has been no time to consider the findings of any overall report, even the broad outlines of which have yet to be formulated. If there is to be a detailed examination of the Party structure, it is conceivable that there may be both majority and minority reports. Surely the proper procedure would be for each of these reports to be presented at every affiliated Union Conference, preferably by spokesmen who had been involved in drafting them? Every Union Conference would then hear all the arguments, and vote in the light of them. Failure to encourage such a debate would mean that crucial questions affecting the organization of the entire Labour movement would be taken arbitrarily, since Trade Union officials, many of whom were direct beneficiaries of quangos and similar governmental perquisites, would be compelled to cast their votes before they had taken the pulse of their own memberships' opinions."[8]

Membership Rights

The matters which concerned the Labour Party's special Committee of Enquiry into its structure and organization included a wide range of problems, from financial difficulties up to the constitutional relationships of the Party with its representatives. But none of these questions can be consistently treated unless we begin with a consideration of the membership of the Party. Such a consideration must turn on the establishment of a clear understanding of those rights and duties which are based upon membership. When a person joins the Party, he or she is entitled to expect that the participatory responsibilities he or she voluntarily shoulders should be matched by a number of entitlements to a due share in influencing the direction of the organization, the determination of its policies and personnel, and the criticism and correction of its performance.

To discuss the membership of the Labour Party is difficult because it comprises two categories. One the one side, individual members are recruited into local Branches which are affiliated to Constituency organizations. It would be simple to draw up a list of the rights and duties of such individual members, and their constitutional position in the Party is relatively clear.

This cannot be said for the other category of membership, which consists of affiliated members. Such members belong to organizations which joined in the federal national movement that created first the Labour Representation Committee and then the Labour Party as we know it at present.

During its first years, this federation consisted of a growing number of trade unions and two or three socialist societies: it had no individual members. The decision to establish individual membership was in fact at first very unpopular with the socialist societies which had helped to found the Party, since they felt the loyalty of their own membership might be threatened by the innovation. For some time, areas in which the ILP was strong were prone to feel this tension. Today, affiliated bodies fall into two groupings. More than six million affiliated members come from the Trade Unions, while the small socialist societies associate a few thousand. Together with the Royal Arsenal Co-operative Society, which is lumped with them because there is nowhere else to put it, this lesser grouping is represented both at the Annual Conference and by one member who serves on the NEC. The Unions carry an overwhelming majority of the votes at policy conferences, and the preponderant influence in determining the Party's leadership.

There is no reason to doubt that the socialist societies do in fact organize the restricted numbers they claim, and are represented accurately at appropriate levels within the constitution of the Party. But this cannot be said of the Trade Unions. If the individual qualifying characteristic of affiliated membership is payment of the political levy, we find very wide variations in the extent to which unions affiliate on precise numbers of intending members. This matter was accurately reported in *Labour Weekly*, when Martin Linton conducted an authoritative survey in 1979.[9]

"The size of the political levy varies enormously from union to union, and so does the amount collected.

NATSOPA and NATTKE, for instance, charge only 20 p a year (5 p a quarter) and since this does not even cover the cost of affiliation to the Labour Party, which is 28 p this year, they have no choice but to affiliate on less than their levy-paying memberships.

NATTKE will be trying to raise their political levy this year, but many unions are rebuffed year after year at their annual conferences when they try to raise the levy.

More than half the unions in the table have not raised their levies since 1977, the year to which the table relates, but some have succeeded, including TASS, who now charge £1.08, SLADE (£1.04), POEU (96p), GMWU (70p), UCATT (52p), AUEW Engineering (50p) and EETPU (35p).

The unions with low political levies (less than 1p a week) had little dificulty in collecting them. NATSOPA, NATTKE, UCATT, UPW, and AUEW Engineering collected 100 per cent. TGWU, EETPU and COHSE collected around 90 per cent.

But the NUR, with a levy of £1 a year, collected only 60p on average. The GMWU charged 60p in 1977, but succeeded in colecting only 35p, though that is still more than many other unions.

Some of the differences may stem from the system of collection. For example, NATSOPA has a flat-rate subscription of 50 a month, and every third month the last 5 p of the subscription is paid into the political fund. To avoid paying the levy, its members would have to pay only 45 p in March, June September and December.

In ASTMS, on the other hand, the levy is paid as a supplement to the normal subscription, so members have to remember to pay the extra £1.20 at the end of the year, or an extra 10p a month. It is easy to forget or to decide not to pay.

This helps to explain why NATSOPA collects 100 per cent of its levy and ASTMS collected only a third (34 per cent) in 1977. ASTMS have 147,000 eligible to pay the levy, and it is impossible to say whether a third pay the full levy or they all pay 40p.

And again, ACTT publish no figure for the number "contracted out". They have the highest political levy, £1.56 a year, and they divide the sum collected by the levy to reach a figure of 1,850 levy-payers. But many more may be eligible to pay the levy.

However, there is yet another complication. Once the union has collected the political levy, it does not necessarily affiliate that number of members to the Labour Party. It may affiliate more, or fewer, in some cases far fewer, but rarely the actual number who pay the levy.

The most famous example is the Transport & General Workers' Union which has over 2 million members but affiliates to The Labour Party on just over 1 million.

This does not cheat the Labour Party out of any money, since all the cash in the political fund has to be spent for political purposes, and nearly all of it goes to the Labour Party in the end. The TGWU has separate regional political funds and makes very big contributions at the regional level.

It does, of course, cheat itself out of votes at the Labour Party conference. It could have nearly 2 million. But the union does not seem keen to press the point.

However, there are many other unions that are affiliated on much less than their levy-paying membership. COHSE affiliated on only 39 per cent of its maximum, though the union says: "That is historical and its in the process of being put right."

NATSOPA and NATTKE affiliate on 32 per cent and 29 per cent of their maximum, and NGA on 44 per cent. But no one is complaining about the way the fund is spent. The NGA, for instance, helps pay for a Labour Party agent at Basildon.

The EETPU made a deliberate decision to scale down its affiliation at national level and increase it at regional level when they failed to win a seat on Labour's NEC.

The POEU spends some of its political fund on its own political education. They run day schools and weekend schools in conjunction with Labour Party regions, which they regard as a contribution "in kind".

Although most unions charge some administrative expenses against their political fund, NUPE is unusual in charging 22½ per cent for the cost of collecting the levy and a further 20 per cent for central administrative expenses.

In 1977 they collected £486,000 of which £105,000 went in central affiliations to the Labour Party, £109,000 in collection costs and £97,000 in administrative expenses. "We apply proper accounting rules to it," says the union. "Really it's lower than we should charge."

UCATT and ASTMS are the only unions that affiliate automatically on the exact number who pay, or are eligible to pay, the levy. The UPOW and SLADE affiliate on 103 and 106 per cent respectively, largely because they are using the previous year's figures when they pay the affiliation fees.

The NUR contrives to affiliate on 110 per cent. "We affiliate on a round number," says the union. "I don't suppose the Labour Party are ungrateful."

There is no real contradiction in this. Those members who do not pay the political levy cannot be charged for Labour Party affiliation, since their money does not go into the political fund. It simply means that these unions spend a little more in central affiliations and a little less in grants, regional affiliations and the like.

The picture that emerges at the end is still a very complex one."

"Complex" is a limited description to apply to the labyrinthine intricacies of this situation. The *Labour Weekly* survey offered the following tabulation of the key issues for a restricted sample of affiliates:

It reveals that several unions have fixed a personal levy which is not only, as Martin Linton points out, lower than the cost of affiliating a single member to the Party at the National level, but also far below the multiple additional costs of participation at subordinate levels. Yet this does not at all fully explain many decisions to affiliate on

	How many in Union? Total union membership (1977) COTUEA*	How many contract out? Contracted out or exempt from political levy (1977)		How many pay levy? Membership paying political levy (1977)		How much do they pay? Political levy collected in total and per member		How many affiliate? Membership affiliated to Labour		How much do they pay? Labour Party dues paid in total and per member		Labour share of max? No. affiliated as per cent of no. paying levy
	Total	Total	%	Total	%	All	Each	Total	%	All	Each	
NUPE	693,097	10,280	1½	682,817	98½	£486,036	£1	500,000	72	£105,000	21p	73 per cent
GMWU	945,324	19,214	2	926,110	98	£324,733	60p	650,000	69	£136,500	21p	69 per cent
TGWU	2,022,738	29,073	1½	1,962,615	97	£570,817	32p	1,074,000	53	£225,540	21p	55 per cent
NUR	171,825	7,605	4½	164,059	95½	£99,166	£1	180,000	105	£37,800	21p	110 per cent
UPW	197,247	10,564	5½	186,683	94½	£84,000	45p	191,967	97	£40,313	21p	103 per cent
COHSE	211,636	18,014	8½	193,622	91½	£38,760	24p	75,000	35	£15,750	21p	39 per cent
NATSOPA	53,396	2,745	5	48,011	90	£9,603	20p	15,220	29	£3,196	21p	32 per cent
EETPU	432,628	44,746	10	364,881	84	£80,173	25p	260,000	60	£54,600	21p	71 per cent
AUEW Eng	1,173,000	297,686	25	875,314	75	£350,686	40p	876,715	75	£184,110	21p	100 per cent
APEX	146,385	37,591	26	108,794	74	£63,264	52p	101,858	70	£22,230	21p	94 per cent
POEU	122,564	33,922	28	88,642	72	£77,971	84p	78,500	64	£16,485	21p	88 per cent
UCATT	305,727	105,727	35	200,000	65	£64,000	32p	200,000	65	£42,000	21p	100 per cent
FBU	40,081	14,617	36	25,464	64	£10,932	52p	16,000	40	£3,360	21p	63 per cent
NATTKE	17,966	7,966	44	10,000	56	£2,000	20p	2,857	16	£600	21p	29 per cent
AUEW Tass	183,492	97,756	53	85,736	47	£49,726	72p	77,522	42	£16,279	21p	90 per cent
NGA	109,438	60,714	55	48,724	45	£11,102	52p	21,464	20	£4,507	21p	44 per cent
ASTMS	441,000	294,000	67	147,000	33	£60,156	£1.20	147,000	33	£30,870	21p	100 per cent
SLADE	25,246	16,963	67	8,283	33	£4,371	52p	8,821	35	£1,852	21p	106 per cent
ACTT	19,974			1,850	9	£2,877	£1.56	1,500	8	£315	21p	81 per cent

* Certification Office for Trade Unions and Employers Associations

memberships far smaller than those which actually contribute to the levy.

Still less does it explain what actual personal political rights correlate with the acceptance of the social duty to contribute to the levy. This is a crucial question, and if the Labour Movement is reluctant to ask it, it will be vulnerable not only to criticism, but also to attack.

Not only is it impossible to establish any consistently applicable body of personal membership rights which attach to payment of the political levy: even collective rights are attenuated, since so many unions are depriving themselves of votes which truly reflect their actually gathered income from the levy, while the processes of internal political policy determination and political activity, vary, according to rule, and also by custom and practice, between one organization and the next.

Since rule changes were brought in during 1965,[10] the status of any trade unionist who agrees to pay the levy, but who refrains from taking out individual membership has in fact amounted to little more than that of a taxpayer: this is because almost all the rights of active membership of the Party have been officially confined, by decision of the 1965 Party Conference, to persons paying full individual membership subscriptions in addition to their political levy. Before that date affiliated members, provided they had not disqualified themselves under rules governing proscribed bodies, or by association with oppositional parties, were entitled to participate at each level of Party organization, serving on Management Committees, City and other Party local government federations, and annual conferences, without ever being compelled to become individual members. Now the only rights conferred on affiliated members by virtue of their payments are rights exercised through their collectives, and these vary significantly from one organization to another. Some are very small indeed. While some unions have an active and lively internal political life, others, to put it gently, are rather torpid.

It seems reasonable to seek to determine some guiding principles under which affiliated members should have clearly determined rights.

First, at the collective level, surely no-one who pays the levy should be unrepresented: affiliates should therefore be obliged to pay on behalf of all who do not contract out.

Second, it may seem reasonable to allow all those who pay to participate at some relevant levels of the Party's organization, as they could before 1966. But it is hardly reasonable that such participation should carry equal rights with individual membership, which now involves a subscription ten times higher than the levies collected by the Party from its affiliates.

Therefore a financial voting system might seem appropriate, under which corporate affiliates cast a vote one tenth as heavy as that of individual members. This could apply at local, Constituency, City or County, Regional and National levels. Its effect would be to modify the block vote so as to reduce the preponderance of large organizations, whilst protecting major trade union interests. It might also encourage many affiliated members to take out full individual membership, rather more actively than has the 1965 reform. If such a new reform were not thought acceptable, the only reasonable alternative would be to seek to codify the rights associated with payment of the levy, within affiliated bodies themselves.

Thirdly, there appears to be some need to collect and compare evidence about the internal mechanisms which have been evolved by affiliated bodies in order to facilitate their members' participation in Party affairs. For instance, one of the residual rights of affiliated trade union branches is that they may nominate persons who wish to be considered for selection at Constituency Selection Conferences for Parliamentary candidates. Some such branches exercise this right after convening their own full scale selection meetings, and interviewing a choice of possible nominees. Others make nominations without any such preliminaries. Some merely pass on names from their union's panel of prospective choices, while others again nominate individuals whose names have been mentioned at an appropriate branch meeting. Some branches are authorized to pay their delegates for attendance at Party management committees, which may become a questionable practice at a time when a selection conference is in the offing. The point is that there is no generally approved code of practice. Of course, any such code should be designed to increase active involvement, not to restrict it. But if it were agreed that affiliated branches should normally interview candidates before nominating them, this could increase real political participation within some branches, whilst diminishing the number of nominations overall, since some who presently nominate would be unwilling to do so if the act involved additional effort on their part.

What applies at the local level appears to apply with less force at the level of national organization. What rules determine the composition of affiliated bodies' delegations to Conferences? What powers do delegations exercise? It is rather clear that different conventions are applied in different organizations. It would be difficult to generalize from these variant experiences in order to determine any applicable body of general collective membership rights which correlate with payment of the political levy.

Up to now the main union responses to discussion of Labour Party finances have emphasized, as has the GMWU in its evidence to the Enquiry on Labour Party Organization, that it is difficult to increase the weight of the political levy in the overall balance of union subscriptions. Rates of levy, that is to say, may only be augmented in the process of increasing general subscriptions with inflation. This may well be a justified assumption. But the more obviously the payment of levy becomes a simple tax on union members, the more justified the assumption will be likely to become. At the same time, hostile attempts to encourage contracting out will increase and the less the rights which attach to payment of the levy, the greater the success which is likely to attend such efforts.

If we suppose that affiliated members should have their status clarified, it becomes possible to set a series of rights and duties which might apply to *all* members, whether affiliated or individual, although such rights may be exercised differently in the separate categories of membership. First, membership entails the right to a share in the determination of policy, either through the criticism of existing policy of performance, or through the development of constructive alternative proposals. Policy may be influenced by simple resolutions, or by more elaborate submissions to relevant committees. The right to determine policy applies at local, constituency, regional and national levels. Secondly, membership entails the right to an appropriately weighted voice in the election of relevant spokesmen at all the above levels in the Party's structure, from management committee through to annual National Conference. Thirdly, membership entails the right to participate directly in the selection of appropriate candidates to represent the Party in electoral contests, from Parish Council through to Parliamentary elections. This particular right might be restricted to nomination or extended beyond this, if the constitution were changed. But no change in the constitution towards enabling greater participation in selection conferences is logically possible without prior reform in the field here discussed, unless affiliated members are to be effectively excluded. Fourthly, membership entails the duty to support the Party financially, to work for it in relevant ways, to abide by its democratic rules and to support it against its opponents. The listing of rights and duties is probably uncontentious. Other rights and duties might well be added, but they would probably generate some controversy. For instance, members might well expect to have their democratic rights made enforceable by an appropriately autonomous disciplinary system. This is an issue which has been discussed at various levels in the Party, and remains unresolved. It is not important when the Party regulates its affairs with a tolerant disposition, but it would become important if policy were to be interpreted rigidly as has sometimes happened in the past.

In the light of a charter of membership rights, we may evaluate the teeming proposals for the reform of party structure rather differently than they have often been evaluated in the recent past. First of all, in relation to leadership, every proposal which complicates the direct accountability of leaders to members is an impediment to democracy. Leaders need to be directly elected by their relevant memberships, and the most obvious and sensible criteria for such elections turn around policy discussions. It may therefore seem quite inappropriate to have an over-sectionalized national leadership. Whether a person represents the Party as a Member of Parliament, a Councillor, a School Governor, or a member of a Health Authority is an accidental question within the Party itself compared to the fundamental question of his or her membership. If members are to exercise differential rights according to the public offices they hold, then the principle of the equality of membership disappears and the democracy of the Party is in jeopardy. MPs discharge their constitutional function inside Parliament, where they must have an appropriate status to do this effectively. Outside Parliament, they should have the general public status they have earned, whether in Party organisations or other voluntary bodies. The responsibility of serving in the Legislature does not entitle one to legislate outside it. If it did, parliamentarians would become semi-feudal grandees.

The same argument applies within the affiliated section of membership. It is in fact the case that the majority of trade union representatives on the present NEC are either Members of Parliament or full-time employees of their unions' head offices. It would be possible to argue that there should be spaces reserved in this section for shop stewards, branch officials, dues collectors or various other categories of membership. Such arguments would be analogous to those seeking representation for, say, councillors, as a special category. They are not acceptable proposals. It is more important to ensure that the electoral processes which determine the membership of the Executive do involve a real degree of membership influence within each affiliated organization, than it is to attempt to legislate for a precise mix of responsibilities and experiences.

The simplest structure for the National Executive, if it is directly to reflect the membership of the Party, is one involving parity between individual members and affiliated members. It would seem to be invidious to seek to tell either category of membership whether it should choose activists working in national or local affairs, or having any other exceptional characteristics.

Footnotes

1. *Tribune*, 6.10.1978, page 7.
2. *Guardian,* Blackpool Diary, 4.10.1978
3. *Tribune*, ibid
4. Allen and Unwin, pp. 289-290.
5. Minkin: *The Labour Party Conference*, p. 197
6. Ibid, p. 198.
7. *The Guardian*, 3 September, 1979.
8. *Workers' Control*, The Bulletin of the IWC.
9. *Labour Weekly*, 8.6.1979.
10. Prior to 1965, the rule governing ward committees read as follows: *"A Ward Committee shall be established in each Ward of the Constituency. Membership shall consist of individual members of this Party, and such members of affiliated societies as enrol themselves as members of a Ward Committee. Individual members and affiliated members must either reside in or be registered as Parliamentary or Local Government electors in the Ward in which they desire to act.*

The Executive Committee of this Party shall endeavour to secure lists of members of affiliated organisations and provide such members with opportunities for enrolment as individual members of this Party, or as members of Ward Committees.

A Ward Committee shall maintain the necessary machinery for elections within its area, and, with the approval of the Executive Committee of this Party: shall undertake propaganda work."

The Annual Conference at Blackpool agreed the following amendment moved by D.H. Davies for the National Executive Committee:

"Line 4: Delete all after '*Party*' up to and including '*Committee*' on line 6.

Lines 6 and 7: Delete the words '*and affiliated members.*'

Lines 14 and 15. Delete the words '*or as members of Ward Committees.*'

With corresponding amendments to Model Rules, Sets C, E, F and G."

This was overwhelmingly carried against an opposition of only 44,000.

At the same time, attendance at the Labour Party Conference, which had previously been open to affiliated members who

"individually accept and conform to the Constitution, programme, principles and policy of the Labour Party and the rules of this Party"

was thenceforward restricted to individual members of the Party. This reform aroused greater opposition. 295,000 votes were cast against it.

CHAPTER TEN

The Forward March
of Labour Halted?

Eric Hobsbawm is a distinguished scholar, a historian profoundly learned in Marxism, and an original thinker. A collection of essays* provoked by his analysis of the present state of the Labour movement ought to be an exciting event. In point of fact, however, it is depressing and discouraging. Raymond Williams, in one of the essays included in the book pinpoints its first problem, which lies in the central metaphor of the keynote contribution around which it has been assembled. The title *The Forward March of Labour Halted?* implies a single unilinear progress where in fact there have been a series of movements, some of which we may reasonably judge to have been "forward", and some of which have not, in any sense, shared that direction. If we seek to determine which way "forward" lies, it can presumably be agreed that it is in the development of demands for a fundamental and irreversible shift of the balance of wealth and power in favour of working people and their families. This involves fostering, however tentatively, hegemonic aspirations in the working-class movement. But since every labour movement only generates this kind of thrust on a basis of proven capacity to defend and advance the corporate interests of those it represents, a large part of its activity commonly does not directly conduce to the growth of specifically socialist goals. If there exist clear-headed socialist perspectives, widely shared, then actions which grow out of the narrowest defensive choices may be transformed in their meaning: but by contrast, where large mass movements erupt without such perspectives, they frequently leave behind little tangible advance towards socialism. If sectionalism in trade unions were in fact as decisive a problem as Hobsbawm's opening essay alleges, then the scope for 'marches' in diverse directions — forwards, backwards, or standing still — would be all that much greater. We shall return to this problem: but to begin with, it must be established that for us, if direction can

* *The Forward March of Labour Halted?* Eric Hobsbawm, with numerous other contributors. Verso, in association with *Marxism Today*, £2.95.

only be a political criterion, then Hobsbawm's own concluding remarks do not contribute to any forward movement whatsoever, still less a march.

To tell us what is already a commonplace assumption, that the social democratic schism in Labour's parliamentary leadership "represents the loss of a significant section of the left-of-centre middle class, which long looked to Labour" is to offer myopic sociology and worse politics. Nowadays local Labour Party organizations are commonly dominated by middle-class people from the caring social services. Probation officers, teachers, welfare workers: these are people who stand in a close relationship with traditional "working class" workers. Rapidly the Labour Party is becoming an organization of persons for whom workers are clients. This explains the large circulation success of *The New Socialist* magazine, which was immediately welcomed by such a readership. All the surveys tell us that the SDP by contrast, is recruiting a different middle class: authoritarian, arbitrary, and nasty towards the unions. What Hobsbawm writes does not help us to assess, still less recoup our loss, to meet which we need a considered and practical response: while to present the 1981 argument in the Labour Party simply as "mutual laceration" without seeking to explain all this "to the satisfaction" of people who remember when the Beatles broke up and have forgotten, as Hobsbawm says, when the Saltley pickets won, is not the conduct of a marcher, forward or otherwise. Such commentary comes from a bystander, albeit a clever and sympathetic one. Hobsbawm does in fact ask some useful questions, many of which have already been asked by other bystanders, some of whom would be far less regretful than he if the march were in fact to stop. But he leaves would-be marchers to find their own answers, and proclaims no great optimism about their capacity to do so.[1] There are, however, grounds for a different view. This can best be approached by looking at the political issues which Hobsbawm's treatment omits to examine.

Most crucially, Hobsbawm's original contribution leaves out all examination of the international dimension of Labour politics. These cannot be reduced to the level of "foreign policy", but also comprehend a whole mesh of far more significant structural links, outside which the current trauma in the Labour Party remains impenetrable to analysts, benign or otherwise. Let us begin with the obvious. The social-democratic "split" which has carried off life peers and Members of Parliament in perceptible numbers, but has not detached one single Party Branch, leave alone constituency organization, and which is nowhere near to disaffiliating even the most oligarchic of union organizations, has consisted almost entirely of members of the "European" faction, originally organized in the Labour Committee for Europe. The secretary of this body, Jim Cattermole, together with Messrs. Jenkins, Williams, Owen and Rogers, assembled the core of this breakaway. Quite possibly some humane people, not only from the middle classes, have rallied to the new organization. But the real ground of the founding schism was commitment to the EEC, and in British circumstances this commitment is one that cannot possibly be shared by a mass movement of working people, whose unions face the destruction of one sector after another of their employment in a competition which none of them can win. The SDP does not even threaten to form a workers' party, and is apparently seeking, if not receiving large business endowments from that multinational sector for which the EEC is indeed a "forward march". That a Labour Party could appeal to some small capitalists, if it evolved political options sufficiently open, is beyond doubt:* but no Labour Party could win any credibility at all in that vast constituency to which it naturally addresses itself, if it sought to ignore the threat to all those marginal enterprises which are about to follow those already being blown away in a gale of EEC competition.

Of course, the Labour argument about the EEC is often conducted within a messy framework of chauvinistic assumptions. The gluiest sentiments to be found in this field, however, come not from the left, but from the solid centre right: it is the Shores and Silkins who topple most easily into a little-England swamp. On the left, Tony Benn's Lisbon speech about the regeneration of Europe provides a welcome contrast.[2] This far-seeing text raises the whole question of the cold-war division of Europe, and opens perspectives far wider than those of EEC orthodoxy.

In any case, Labour has now lost its hard-core Europeans. Nobody on the left has said that this is a "good riddance", largely because the culture of a broad church goes along with the widespread acceptance of the catholic doctrine "hate the sin but not the sinner". Yet cold-blooded agnostic analysis, of the kind at which Hobsbawm hints but fails to provide, surely indicates that there has been a certain

---

* For instance, it could help small shopkeepers against the big combines, by planning for decentralised shopping centres instead of hypermarkets. But slum clearance during the last two decades has strangled small family businesses faster than it has spawned new Wimpey estates. Miles of small shops have given place to colossal high-rent shopping areas, and usually with heavy support from Labour Councillors.

inevitability about this process. Hard-headed political scrutiny, surely, would indicate that there are other squared circles which are liable to flip roundly back to shape as current political crises take their course. Preeminent among these is the Atlanticist crisis. This could not have been more completely encapsulated than it was in Labour's deputy leadership campaign, where Tony Benn defended Labour's main policy commitments, including that to thoroughgoing nuclear disarmament, against Denis Healey who made it public that he would not "serve" in a unilateralist Labour Government. Denis Healey's television threat meant very plainly that he (and presumably a large part of the parliamentary caucus which supports him) would seek to wreck the implementation of the major international policy which has crystallised in the Labour movement since the defeat of 1979. More: in any narrowly-hung parliament, this ploy would be successful. Labour could then only govern if it abandoned its policies. While it is quite proper to argue with Denis Healey, and to seek to win over his supporters, and whilst many will hope that the force of argument will ultimately persuade most of the defenders of Atlanticism, it requires a remarkable degree of self-deception to imagine that this fundamental disagreement can be simply papered over. It would be more realistic to see the present division of social democrats into European exitists and Atlantic remainers as a division of labour in the sense of Adam Smith: or a hedging of bets. Those who go seek to "break the mould" and establish a new capitalist managerial party; while those who stay seek to neutralise Labour's response, and sabotage its victories if that ever becomes necessary.

Any rigorous discussion of the tendency of the Labour movement in Britain would need to go to the roots of Denis Healey's commitment, which has been, over the three decades since the formation of NATO, inextricably meshed into the perspectives of the Atlantic Alliance.[3] This commitment is in no way reducible to such positions as have subsequently been evolved in the Italian Communist Party, whose relatively recent recognition of NATO emerged as the reluctant acceptance of an accomplished fact. Denis Healey, as a talented protege of Ernest Bevin, a shaper of the postwar European settlement, was not merely a spectator, but an architect, of the process which solidified the two main blocs, and deliberately set out to extinguish any option for non-alignment, leave alone autonomous action, by the working class movement of Europe. This vast polarisation it was which halted Labour's "forward march" in the early 'fifties, and locked European socialism into stagnation and sterility for decades. The alibi that the postwar boom necessarily invalidated socialist choices will not stand up. On the contrary, if ever there were conditions in which peaceful change was optimally possible, and broadening prospects of radical reform could have been consensually accepted, it was during the long boom years that these conditions most evidently applied. But European socialists were divided into opposing orthodoxies which choked out all hope of basic structural change in the interests of working people.

As the head of the International Department at Transport House during the immediate postwar years, Denis Healey played an absolutely crucial role in the rebirth of the Socialist International, and in the earlier organization of Comisco, which was the liaison committee which brought the various socialist parties into close enough relations with one another to facilitate this rebirth. But this delicate process of realignment did not take place in a vacuum, and was very far from being a simple restoration of the prewar links. In every European Labour Movement after 1945 there existed substantial groupings of socialists sharing independent international perspectives. The evolution of the Cominform, which was quite visible in public, turned around the thesis of "two camps" which was developed by Andrei Zhdanov, and which had the immediate intention of solidifying Soviet influence and control in the countries of Eastern Europe. Heads rolled, and quickly: not only social democrat heads, but all independent socialist heads and hundreds of alleged "national" communist ones.[4] The effect of this policy in Western Europe was to assist in stifling all "third force" trends, and to consolidate the alignment of Western Europe with the United States. This alignment involved a very active, if much less visible, American input, and nowhere more than in the field of European Labour Politics. The Central Intelligence Agency, however, was only formed in the dawning years of the cold war, and a key role in the elaboration of the Western version of "two camps" fell to Ernest Bevin in the foreign office and his assistants in the British Labour Party; particularly to Denis Healey.

During these years the split in the World Federation of Trade Unions was followed by splits in a number of national trade union centres, and there is strong evidence of outside intervention in this process. If there was good reason for unions to oppose stalinist caucuses in the Federation, there were no defensible reasons for substituting them by CIA patronage. That is why the many very damaging CIA activities were all covert. But at the same time, there were also substantial external pressures on the political parties of the European left. These may be seen most clearly in the Italian socialist movement, where they ultimately succeeded not only in levering a NATO-aligned social democratic party into being, but also in weakening the support for autonomous policies in the main socialist organization at the same time.[5] After the Socialist International was reborn, the trend continued. Neutral voices were restrained and isolated. The establishment of the Bilderburg group in 1954, the development of "revisionism" of the varieties of the German SDP's Bad Godesburg programme and C. A. R. Crosland's major work *The Future of Socialism*, were all part of the same process which gave us the foundation of the Congress for Cultural Freedom as a CIA response to Stalin's intellectual "Peace" movements. On both sides, this was the politics of cynical manipulation, and many of the participants involved were simply naive. Some, however, knew what they were at.

It would be absurd to rehearse this story in order to score points off the surviving individual contenders in it, for all that. The postwar alignment of Europe was a tragedy, in which good men fell into traps on both sides. Some later recovered better judgement. A nuanced history of European Labour would involve a need for charity and much complexity. Our point here is more basic: the development of socialist movements in Europe was arrested partly by direct subversion, partly by indigenous obstacles, but mainly by the emergence of a new world balance during this awful time, in which many formerly autonomous working class movements of Europe were aligned and incorporated in the services of competing blocs, within the shade of whose rivalry there was no conceivable long-term possibility of advancing Labour's control over the political process. Eastern oriented parties apologized for inexcusable atrocities and flatly denied the existence of Gulag. Western oriented parties progressively abandoned more and more of their social aspirations as they closed ranks to become part of a political-military system which was deeply hostile both to socialism, however libertarian; and to neutralism, however even-handed. The very concepts of left and right were, for the contending apparatchiks of both sides, subsumed into the geopolitical categories of East and West. Hobsbawm himself paid part of the price for this remorseless deterioration. So did an entire generation. And all this happened at a moment when the Labour Party in Britain began to live through the "thirteen wasted years", losing successive elections, and yet maintaining very high levels of membership and apparent organizational vitality. This vitality ensured strong defence of the corporate interests of the working class, but it was confined within a national framework which had unobtrusively surrendered crucial powers to the institutions of the Western block, and, at the same time, and far more damagingly, surrendered the vision of any alternative destiny.

It has only been as this closed system began to crumble that socialist options became thinkable in one European country after another. The long-term re-emergence of the French left depended on the recovery of a certain rather marked autonomy from the alliance system by the French state, under de Gaulle. The very conflicts provoked by de Gaulle's domestic ascendancy gathered their transformational potential from the fact that France was not totally locked into the alliance system. The recovery of political democracy in the former fascist states of Portugal and Spain, and in Greece, gave further momentum to the recovery of autonomous working class objectives in the other nations of the West. The upsurge of socialism with a human face in Czechoslovakia, and then of Solidarity in Poland, opened new possibilities of insight both East and West, and increased the strains in Eurocommunism, which itself is a reaction to the same underlying trends. Whether all this will become a "forward march" in a co-ordinated convergence it is too early to say: but it is surely difficult to deny that it profoundly affects the mid-term prospects of the British left.

We should not ignore another way of viewing these developments. Did not the cold war division of Europe actually foment militarist subversion in Greece and prolong Iberian fascism even beyond the point where it had become so attenuated that it was ready to collapse in upon itself?

And is there not another lesson to be drawn from these experiences of European socialism? Only yesterday, after the fall of the Colonels in Greece, the leftwing socialist 'neutralist' PASOK polled 13% of the vote. In 1981 the government of Andreas Papandreou was installed, upon an unambiguous programme of the left, with the direct support of 47% of the Greek electors, whilst more than three-fifths of the voters supported one left-wing party or another; an absolute majority. Similarly, the compromised socialism of Guy Mollet and his confreres in France reduced French socialism to the merest rump. Presidential candidates received as little as 6% of the popular vote. The regeneration of the Socialist Party in France depended upon a total renewal, in which even the right-wing (recruited from the independent socialist PSU) made the main axis of its programme hinge upon appeals for self-management and devolution of governmental powers. Having lived through the near-total discredit of the Wilson–Callaghan years, what force will allow the Labour Party to renew itself less traumatically? Whatever answers we evolve to this question, the growth of the European Nuclear Disarmament movement, holding out a specific long-term goal of non-alignment in the whole political territory of Europe, is an augury of considerable promise. It offers an alternative framework, within which national political forces will gain greater freedom of movement, first inside, and later between, the superpower alliances. Of these forces, who can doubt that the Labour and Socialist parties will benefit the most?

I have written a great deal about the apostasies of the Labour Governments of 1964–70 and 1974–79, and much of it agrees with Hobsbawm's concluding remarks in that section of his final essay which dismisses those experiences.[6] In a nutshell, both these administrations began with a number of reforms which defended or restored the corporate defences of the trade unions, and both fell when their response to economic difficulties, and their disorientation, led them to mount open attacks upon those corporate defences. So the baleful Rookes–Barnard judgement provoked remedies, and the Industrial Relations Act was repealed, only to be followed on both occasions by prolonged backsliding.

In this respect, Jack Jones contributes an interesting commentary which deserves to be discussed further. He rightly insists that both *In Place of Strife* during 1969, and the 5% pay policy of 1978 were disasters: and these were precisely the most visible attacks on trade union defensive powers. But the most fundamental onslaught on the corporate powers of Labour was not mounted directly against the unions at all, although it hit them harder than any regressive legislation or restrictive pay policies: it came about with the IMF counter-revolution, which involved a Labour Government in reneging on its fundamental postwar commitment to full employment, in reversing the commitment to welfare, and in major concessions to monetarist prescriptions. This was the practical defeat of social democracy of the Crosland stamp. The argument of this revisionist school had been coherent, and rested on the assumption that full employment was itself an "irreversible shift" in effective working class power. The reversal of this postwar shift nullified the Butskellite consensus, before Mrs. Thatcher's rise to office, and before the birth of the modern Social Democrats, who have abandoned all pretensions to full employment, leave alone "socialism".

But why? We have it on the authority of his widow that Crosland was profoundly distressed by this course of events, and saw them from the beginning as constituting that sea-change which has now, in hindsight, been generally recognized. And yet the IMF terms actually agreed were very close to the Fund's original negotiating position, and much sharper than was 'necessary'. They represented very small if any bargaining advances by the Government, and their fierceness actually surprised some of their IMF proponents who had deliberately left themselves room for manoeuvre which was never taken up.

The most plausible explanation of this strange affair is precisely that the weight of commitment to change in the Labour movement meant that parts of the Callaghan administration saw in the IMF demands a convenient external discipline. Order was being restored. Once again, it came from the international agencies, which politely and firmly set bounds to our otherwise temptingly radical range of internal policy choices. The political face of that new order, the Lib–Lab pact which Jack Jones rightly criticizes, was an augury of what should be expected if ever the Social Democrats are able to come into any future coalition government, except of course that the IMF settlement preceded and guaranteed the disaster of Thatcherism, while whoever wins the next election will inherit a shattered economy, festering social turmoil on all sides, and deep-structured crisis. What Jack Jones offers to face all this will be nothing like enough to restore full employment. His instinct for simple, communicable priorities is a good one, and it is much to be hoped that issues like shorter working hours and a national minimum wage can become rallying points around which unions can begin to deepen the political responses which are the only solid general strategy left to union members who are surrounded by three, rising to four million unemployed former workmates.

But the priority of pensions, imposed upon the 1974 Labour Government after a brilliant campaign led by Jack Jones himself, did not guarantee the success of the structural reforms which the Labour Party had embraced in opposition. Neither did the agreement on the social contract, although the unions went beyond the call of duty to honour this. Since the Government lacked the political will to implement its pledges on industrial democracy, and since Harold Wilson was determined to wreck the Industry Act which promised mandatory planning agreements and active state intervention in economic development, the key political accords which underpinned the social contract were dishonoured. Strong pressure for progress in the spirit of these agreements came from the moderate trade union centre, and notably from those forces led by David Basnett and Clive Jenkins. Clive Jenkins' own union published a draft planning agreement, and sought to school its members in what it saw as a new beginning for trade union involvement in key decisions.

Although Jack Jones himself was the General in another very capably-fought campaign for the implementation of the TUC proposals on industrial democracy, this series of battles ended in a clear defeat. Obviously, it would have been very useful if he could have offered us his analysis of this. In my view, it arose because the trade union left, of which he was the unchallenged leader (by far the most outstanding trade union strategist of our generation) was divorced from the emerging political left. Had the demotion of Tony Benn from the Industry Department been effectively resisted in 1975, perhaps the story could have been different. As things were, Labour Leaders picked off those adversary policies of their own movement which troubled them, one at a time, and dropped them into the pickling buckets for another day. That day did not come.

Precisely this episode provides us with a major illustration of the difficulty of assessing "forward marches". Both the TUC concern for industrial democracy and the Labour Party's industrial programme were seen by their authors as contributions to that "irreversible shift of wealth and power to working people and their families" which was proclaimed in Labour's 1973 programme. The pre-eminent Labour Parliamentary leadership shared no commitment at all to this objective: their concern both between 1964 and 1970, and again after 1974, was to stabilise the existing order at whatever degree of adverse balance proved requisite. Eric Hobsbawm does not wish us to describe this tension as a "betrayal", and we may perhaps respect his sensitivities. At best it was a salutary lesson in perfidy. The least that can be said about it is that these manoeuvres involved some highly intricate, indeed balletic, countermarching: with the membership pressing tentatively, apprehensively forward, and the preponderent leadership beating a stiff tattoo and striding purposively in the opposite direction. Jack Jones showed extraordinary political skill in marshalling the TUC for the modest reform proposals of the Bullock Committee, which would, to be sure, have had one profoundly beneficial effect for the shop stewards he consistently defended. They would have enabled effective combine committees, with real teeth, to come into operation in every major company. But he was outflanked, first by Harold Wilson and then by James Callaghan, who deployed the far lesser talents of Edmund Dell and Shirley Williams against him, and successfully shredded his entire programme. From their new vantage-point in the SDP, these partisans of management's divine rights now have the gall to speak of the need for "more industrial democracy". Treachery or not, we are bound to note that the Society of Dishonest Politicians has gathered into its new ranks by no means all the most skilful practitioners who were schooled in those forlorn administrations. But no doubt the work of realignment will continue.

Jack Jones would have been interesting, too, if he had further taken up Hobsbawm's thoughts on "sectionalism". The most striking example of a united class response given by contributors to this book's discussion was that of the 1972 dockers' boycott of container depots, which brought the National Industrial Relations Court (and the Tipstaff of the High Court) to ultimate humiliation, after five dockers had been arrested and sent off to prison. The mass strike which was then impending did not actually have to happen, because the whole machinery of state suddenly apprehended the danger confronting it. Yet never was there a more "sectional" dispute than this, where dockers were opposing the transfer of their work to container-loaders, all organized in the ranks of the same trade union.

On the other side, the social contract scarcely reeks of sectionalism. And yet Jack Jones is right (and his critics err) on the evaluation of the earliest phases of that arrangement.

Michael Barratt Brown has provided a careful study of what happened to the distribution of the national income during the period 1974–79, a period of "almost nil growth". During this time, improvements in low pay obviously meant reductions in the standards of others, and as Barratt Brown pointed out "this in fact meant cuts in better paid workers' incomes, as well as increased taxes on the rich". Having said this, 1975 "marked a high point in the share of wages and salaries in British National Income".[7]

Taking income shares as a percentage of gross national product at factor cost, employee compensation moved from 70.6% in 1974 to 73.5% in 1975. Then, after Mr. Wilson's counter-revolution which followed the 1975 referendum on British membership of the EEC, the lid was screwed down, and the figure began to decline: from 71.5% in 1976 down to 69.5% in 1978, approaching the point at which it had become established during the years 1969–73. In other words, during the first phase of the social contract there took place in one year a substantial shift in the distribution of national income towards the working population, within which shift more went to lower paid workers than to higher paid ones. But subsequently, new phases of the contract accompanied a reduction in that proportion of the national income paid out in wages, which came down sharply year by year.

It is not altogether surprising that a majority of trade unionists gave their support to the early phases, and became more and more exasperated as the advantages of the bargain slipped away. There are many lessons to be drawn from this experience, but they are not being discussed very objectively on the left, or anywhere else for that matter. However, one thing which this experience does not reflect is narrow sectionalism. During the year of maximum breakthrough the entire trade union movement was able to bargain as one representative organism. Subsequently it lost out, and this fact is entirely attributable to losses on the political plane. But even when the social contract was collapsing, the collapse did not only result in sectional or sectoral claims. Of course, significant advances had been made in organizing the growing local authority and welfare services and they were able to test their industrial muscle, having been nurtured in the political space gained by trade unionism in the immediately preceding period. But the revolt of the low paid workers was widely supported, if only because it crossed the frontiers between the main general unions. For all that, the legacy of disappointment and disruption left by the social contract did promote a degree of sectionalism, notably among the same skilled workers who were later tempted to vote for the Thatcherite programme of "free collective bargaining". These workers by no means lacked "militancy". In the early 'sixties, some socialists argued that incomes policies would politicise the trade unions, and weld them into overall class bargaining agencies, determining wages as a whole against the overall return to capital, centrally. The truth was to prove more ironical. There is apparently, in the age of incomes policies, a pendulum which swings between centralised and sectional union activities, just as there remains that other pendulum which moves between political and industrial responses. What is not possible is to identify *a priori* the political meaning of sectionalism. Sectionalism would only be a cardinal sin in a consistently syndicalist ground-plan for revolution. In a pluralist democracy, even in one developing towards a socialist (hegemonic) consensus, things will be more complicated.

The 1979 swing to conservatism among trade unionists should have underlined this lesson. Yet the argument for a national minimum wage, and a national maximum, can be divorced from that on incomes policy as a corporate control mechanism, and the left will ignore this at some peril.

But the most dated part of the original debate in *Marxism Today*, with which this book begins, is the discussion on trade unionism. Mass unemployment implies profound changes in trade union behaviour, as well as trade union policy and orientation. These require careful scrutiny and discussion, which has hardly begun.

III

The main political prescription offered by Eric Hobsbawm is that to be effective the Labour Party needs to be able to win elections, and that doctrinal purity is no substitute for this capacity. Since he blongs to a party which is not at all endowed with this potential, it is understandable that he should appreciate its importance. However, unless we agree that doctrine is irrelevant to the needs of voters we cannot afford to ignore it.

The Labour Party in opposition has shown a remarkable degree of unity upon a number of rather clear policies. It is overwhelmingly in favour of leaving the European Economic Community. It supports unilateral nuclear disarmament, but if anything it even more strongly opposes the placement of United States nuclear weaponry in Britain. It desperately wants the restoration of full employment, and if the strategies chosen to achieve this aim do not lack certain contradictory elements, they do reveal a powerful consensus for the extension of direct intervention, planning agreements, local and regional enterprise agencies, and new measures of industrial democracy. And it quite correctly perceives that all these objectives are unattainable if it does not reform the national constitution by abolishing the House of Lords. I suppose all this is doctrine. It is also passionately opposed, item by item, by variable majorities in the Parliamentary Labour Party: but the opposition does not take the form of rational debate, offering refutation of this or that proposed policy. Instead it takes the form of evasion, manipulation, and studied ambiguity. Nobody answers or challenges the left proposals. Instead it is hoped to lose them in packed committees. Indeed, the Social Democratic split itself can be seen preeminently as a device to maintain the capacity to continue such procedures.

Underlying all this is the sombre fact that these reforms imply a direct assault on the major centres of transnational capital, which alone can open the possibility of arriving at any genuine form of parliamentary government, or at any effective defence of local and trade union democracy.

By 1984, there will be a minimum of 4½ million people unemployed, and any recovery in the profitability of industry will increase that number. In short, British capitalism is in permanent, festering, acute crisis. A Labour Party which attempted to administer this would disappear in a convulsive and terminal paroxism. There is no available fudge to avert this truth. Therefore, the problem is not how to placate the parliamentarians who refuse to face facts, but how to reconstitute a political labour movement which is not afraid to meet reality where it is.

Industrial action there will be, but it is extremely improbable that it can in these circumstances displace or even significantly foreshorten political processes. Mass unemployment restricts all trade unions and reduces some to virtual impotence, so they have no generally effective weapon to use in their defence other than that of political action. But the Labour Party has delayed its internal reckoning to a perilously late hour, and cannot, indeed will not be allowed, to postpone it further. Meantime, people riot, and wealth is redistributed by rampaging mobs which shop at night with bricks for store windows. King Mob is already visiting, and this fact alone shows the extent of regression and collapse to which democratic remedies have been subjected.

That is why Tony Benn's campaign for the deputy leadership was an indispensable and minimum response. It revealed many things which need serious discussion, all of which are largely ignored in this book, which for all its merits as a map of the existing left urgently needs to be transcended. First, the intervention of Michael Foot represented an impossible attempt to forestall social democratic breakaways by restraining and fudging the Party's socialist commitments. For perhaps thirty or forty right-wing parliamentarians, the SDP has already become an irresistible option, and their departure is purely contingent on tactical advantage. If it pays them to sit on the Leader's head in order to induce him to do indefensible things, they will sit for just long enough to provoke those things. This will, they hope, induce demoralisation in what they already plainly regard as the enemy camp. The more, they think, the better. They will go tomorrow, the happier if the shambles is the greater. Benn's hair's breadth defeat makes this vicious process the more inevitable. Had he won, or been resoundingly trounced, these issues might have been attenuated. But today, his opponents know, time is not on their side. There is, therefore, likely to be no alternative to a bitter conflict in the Labour Party, in which the leadership itself may soon become a direct and public issue. From the days of Attlee onwards, there arose a tradition that the natural position of Labour leaders was "slightly to the left of centre". Harold Wilson left little life in this but its penumbra of myth. External and internal social democrats must today seek to stifle even this, since it conflicts with their own necessary fictions. These celebrate the "middle ground" at that precise moment when affairs have submerged it beneath ocean depths of unemployment and crisis. If Labour's present leader balks at adjusting to impossible demands from this lobby, they will do what they can to destroy him. If, on the other hand, he agrees to adjust, he will destroy himself. However he chooses, the Party will surely remain turbulent. In this context, Hobsbawm's off-day (as Royden Harrison rightly describes it in the best piece in this book) will quickly be forgotten.

This discussion is based upon an inadequate appreciation of the depth of the crisis in the old Labour Party, as well as a far from adequate appreciation of the impact of the wider political economic crisis on all British institutions. The Labour Party will undoubtedly come through this trauma, and will find the programmatic responses which are necessary to unite the working population and the vast unemployed population, in undertaking the necessary social transformation. To this end, it will need policies which are reasonable as well as radical, balanced and feasible as well as far-reaching. But although the definition of a policy is a crucial task, even more important are the determination to carry it through, and the courage not to run from adversary pressure. We shall have ample scope to develop these qualities in the coming months, and whatever reservations have been expressed by the contributors to this book in their (yesterday's) attempts to make sense of yesterday, we may have good reason to think they will be pleased to join in the forward march now already forming its ranks. Tomorrow is going to be a different story.

Footnotes

1. In fact, numerous forward marchers have already begun to develop their ideas, and some of them can be found in *How to Win*, Spokesman 1981, where there is an extended discussion of problems of democratic planning, workers' alternative plans, local government enterprise, and related issues.
2. See Tony Benn: *European Unity—A New Perspective*, Spokesman Pamphlet 75.
3. We still await an adequate account of these years. Richard Fletcher's paper in *The CIA and the Labour Movement* (Spokesman 1971) covers some of the ground in a balanced way. It is a striking example of newspaper suppression, since it was expensively commissioned by the Sunday Times, only to be excised on editorial instructions. ("These people are our friends", said the editor.) *Trade Unions in Britain* (Spokesman, 1980) contains an account of the international trade union schism. An even more important example of media censorship is to be found in Richard Fletcher's still unpublished UNESCO paper *The Free Flow of News*, on covert political operations in the media under Ernest Bevin's dispensation at the foreign office. The Mayhew papers, filed with *The Observer*, contain vital information on the way in which intelligence officers went to work to orchestrate news coverage, publishing activities, and syndication services in order to manipulate opinion, especially where socialism and neutralism were perceived as threats.

4. The Prague takeover by the Communist Party was the visible cause of the socialist reaction which had been "unthinkable" to most European socialists before. As Braunthal puts it, in his insider account of the development of the International: "the depths of conflict existing between Social Democracy and the Soviet Union which came to a head over the Prague *coup*, explain their attitude to the Brussels Treaty of March 1948, and a year later, to the North Atlantic Treaty . . . the very idea that social democracy might improve an alliance with the capitalist United States against the Soviet Union had been unthinkable before the Prague coup d'etat". (*History of the International*, Gollancz 1980, pp 192-4). However, the evidence of Fletcher, cited above, shows that British Labour Party officials had been thinking the unthinkable for some time before that event. A key paper in the Mayhew archives, dated January 1947, makes this quite clear.

5. The Italian supporters of Saragat, however, took some time to align themselves, and in the earliest days they had an anti-NATO majority. This shows how intractable the socialist movement was to the pressure for bloc alignment.

6. See, for instance, the papers in *What Went Wrong?* Spokesman 1979.

7. Ibid, pp. 59 et seq.

CHAPTER ELEVEN

After Imperialism?

"Empire is no more, and now the Lion and the Wolf shall cease."
William Blake

In 1953 Stalin died. That same year, in January, a second leader in the wartime alliance, President Eisenhower, wrote about a third, Winston Churchill, in his diary. The old man was getting past it, he recorded.

> "He has fixed in his mind a certain international relationship he is trying to establish — possibly it would be better to say an atmosphere he is trying to create. This is that Britain and the British Commonwealth are not to be treated just as other nations would be treated by the United States . . . On the contrary, he most earnestly hopes and intends that those countries shall enjoy a relationship which he thinks will recognize the special place of a partnership they occupied with us during World War II . . . Winston is trying to relive the days of World War II. In those days he had the enjoyable feeling that he and our President were sitting on some rather Olympian platform with respect to the rest of the world . . . In the present international complexities, any hope of establishing such a relationship is completely fatuous . . .
> Much as I hold Winston in my personal affection, and much as I admire him for his past accomplishments . . . I wish that he would turn over leadership of the British Conservation (sic) Party to younger men."[1]

But Winston Churchill was not the only advocate of the "special relationship". At the Morecambe Conference of the Labour Party, the previous October, Denis Healey had put it in as tight little a nutshell as anyone could seek:

> "There are five good reasons why we in Britain have got to work with the Americans as closely as possible for as far as we can see ahead. We cannot solve the Russian problem without America. We cannot solve the German problem without America. We cannot keep the Commonwealth together unless we are friendly with the United States. Finally, we cannot

solve our own economic problems or the problem of poverty in Asia and Africa without the co-operation of the Americans."[2]

Mr. Healey's words evoked an immediate response: as one delegate said, shortly afterwards "I would not have been surprised to hear him say we could not hold this Conference without American co-operation". In fact there was no shortage of such "co-operation" from the Congress for Cultural Freedom and other United States' front organizations, during the tumultuous years of the Bevanite argument. They intervened heavily, and to effect. But there was a great shortage of co-operation on the higher strategic plane, as Ike made abundantly clear his studied indifference to the goal of "keeping the Commonwealth together".

Within three years, the Americans had brought all their considerable influence to bear in Britain in order to bring about the downfall of Eden, as a chastisement for the unauthorized Suez adventure.[3] After an initial but brief chauvinist lapse, Hugh Gaitskell had correctly read the transatlantic indicators, and from that moment onwards he put up an impassioned defence of the special relationship through the climax of that crisis.[4] But the relationship was henceforward to follow the Eisenhower pattern, not the Healey pattern.

Now, after three decades, it is perfectly clear that we have not in this framework solved any of Denis Healey's five problems, with the possible exception of the "German question". Federal Germany has become Europe's most prosperous capitalism, and the German Democratic Republic in Europe's (and the world's) most prosperous "socialism". But both are at the centre of a divided Europe which is more heavily armed, with more lethal weapons systems, than has been any previous confrontation in history.[5] As for the "Russian problem" it remains as intractable as ever: the world superpower arms race has abandoned all pretence at rational policy formation, and is now visibly caught in frenzy.[6] Britain's own economic problems have steadily worsened, the Commonwealth now consists of a thin sprinkle of depopulated islands whose one continuing significance is that they can all apparently involve us in wars which we cannot afford to fight, together with a consortium of independent states which are much more commonly seen apart than "together". As for poverty in Asia and Africa, the only observable contribution of the special relationship has been to make it worse. Whilst the unilateral British aid programme may be given some credit for (very inadequate) good intentions, the strategic demands of the special relationship have all worked the other way. Wars and threats of war have reduced some of the poorest countries in the world to the direst of extremities. Coups and militarist putsches have recurrently nipped in the bud those attempts at radical or revolutionary change which might have brought an end to endemic hunger. Often these have been helped along by the CIA. Usually Britain's role in this part of the relationship has been that of flag-waver, while the Agency or the State Department have done most of the actual dirty work: but from time to time British expertise has been given some modest scope to exert itself, as, for instance, in Iran. Most of the contracts for special equipment and thumbscrews have gone to American firms, although Britain has picked up the odd order for handcuffs.

In practical terms, then, it seems that the Healey programme of 1952 has not produced any very marked advantage to the people who support the Labour Party, unless they are locksmiths. But what of the theory? Coincidentally, it was also in 1952 that there appeared a bright pink volume called *New Fabian Essays*, in which Denis Healey told us that "*Leviathan* is still a better handbook for foreign policy than *Fabian Essays*".[7] "An understanding of the power element in politics," said our present foreign affairs spokesman in Parliament, "is the first necessity for a sound foreign policy". It was no doubt upon this perception that Mr. Healey based his prescription for "co-operation" with the Americans. Close scrutiny of their "power element" would undoubtedly pronounce it to be marked and thus well-deserving of such co-operation. This is normally clad in words about democracy. But Thomas Hobbes taught us to look beneath words to material realities,[8] and if we really followed Denis Healey's advice we would notice, rather quickly, that America's world-wide power structure has rested upon the deployment of truly remarkable economic resources, rather than the export of various admirable but entirely domestic democratic institutions. The verbal excuses for the cold war do not explain the true conflict of those powers which are waging it. Balance sheets, not the Declaration of Rights, determine overseas policy in Washington.

Perhaps this was not completely plain in the 'fifties. But how can it be denied in the 'eighties? United States agencies have directly intervened to overthrow democratic institutions in Iran, Guatemala, Indonesia, Chile, and El Salvador, to name only some outstanding and well-documented cases.[9] That democracy which rules the USA internally, not without contest and challenge, but nonetheless impressively, has been not in the least applicable as an external policy in all such cases as these. And if "democracy" is turned into a declamatory smokescreen for those kinds of arbitrary actions, it is not one whit superior in logic or morality to a "socialism" which has been reduced to operating at bayonet-point through military coups in Poland. Yet of course, however immoral either world bloc may be, Hobbes would be right to remind us that we should pay attention to the effective material powers wielded by them, before worrying overmuch about what they said. But this attention does not entail "co-operation" with the strongest. It might well imply an opposite commitment.

Short-sighted observers told us, throughout the 'thirties, that in a Hobbesian world, the British Empire represented a potent force. Scholars who perceived that the British imperium was sometimes tentative in its reactions began to discuss why it was that there had arisen a paralysis of the imperial will. The truth, however, was different: the will was anything but paralysed, and pursued its often malignant course to the limits of its powers. What was in crisis was the economic strength upon which "will" based its force, and it was potency, not intention, which had been enfeebled. The fact that this "will" survived can be read in these writings of an earlier Denis Healey, who was seeking, in the developing special relationship, the maintenance of as many as possible of those old imperial commitments in a sublimated (and parasitic) form. When Eisenhower caused the downfall of Anthony Eden, the inappropriateness of this hope dawned upon Macmillan, and it was very likely this appreciation that gave us the "Wind of Change" speech on African decolonisation. Even so, it was to take further painful years of useless and expensive procrastination by Labour Governments before the similarly insupportable "East of Suez" commitments could be liquidated.

The recognition of independent Zimbabwe proved beyond Labour's capacity, and, with help from the senior partner in a decreasingly 'special' relationship, was finally accomplished by Lords Carrington and Soames for the Thatcher administration.

Empire is almost no more, and now the Lion and the Wolf have moved to the Falkland Islands. This latest crisis shows us three souls in the Labour Party. One is for peace. The Falklands can not be maintained under British control without eating up large amounts of scarce resources which are desperately needed in the welfare section of the British economy, and nobody can think that 1800 people's half-cancelled nationality gives them the right to shave a regular billion and a half off our denuded school or health budgets. Rather, says this wing of the Party, they should be helped to resettle, or protected by other, negotiated means.

The second soul expresses the simple atavism of Empire, and is heard speaking most clearly in the cardboard Churchillian periods of Peter Shore, whose chauvinism is pure, unaffected, and unrelieved by finer feelings. This soul is also part resident in Michael Foot, when he is not trimming to maintain the affections of his deputy. To have told Mrs. Thatcher, of all people, that she would be judged "by deeds, not words" will not easily be forgiven by a new generation of Britons, who will either be asked to carry the human burdens of failure in the South Atlantic, or the even greater economic burdens of "success". This current of Labour opinion has a long if disreputable history, going back to famous jingoes like Hyndman, or Blatchford, but not going forward to anything. It is moribund, and Labour can only carry it as an incubus. All this current foaming at the mouth would be met with indulgent laughter, if the disgrace of it were not to be exacted in blood.

And the third soul is the Atlanticist soul of Denis Healey, for whom all the transitions have been neatly accomplished. No longer is the Commonwealth to be sustained by co-operation with the Americans, but now co-operation with the Americans requires that Britons take the long view, not to "lose South America" for the sake of two small islands the size of Wales. The new Empire has replaced the old. But not all of us wish to acclaim it. It may not happen, of course, but nothing would suit some of us better than the fall of the Argentine Junta should dominoe throughout the continent, "losing" it to those who set up the academies for training torturers from Brazil through to Guatemala.

Conditions on the Falklands are not likely to be a long-term problem. Soon the weight of international influence will combine with the outcome of battles on the islands to determine their future. The weight of economic adversity in England will play its part in shaping even the truly Hobbesean will of Mrs. Thatcher.

But the future of the Labour Party will be more difficult to manage. Empire's decline, and the swelling of the cold war to fill the space available, have left the British people with a completely false set of policy choices, into which we have been locked over some decades. These are now blown open in an explosion of truths: that deterrence does not deter, that present alliances are skin-deep, that power grows not out of the barrel of a gun, but out of productivity indices and balances of payments. Now the renewal of honest socialist politics absolutely requires the development of genuinely non-aligned policies, and the determination to seek out new allies and realistic relationships, for objectives which are different.

Footnotes

1. This diary entry of 5th January 1953 is cited in David Carlton: *Anthony Eden, a Biography*, Allen Lane, 1981, pp. 332-3.
2. *Labour Party 51st Annual Conference Report*, 1952, p. 123.
3. This story is carefully told in Carlton's biography, notably in Chapter XI. Here, for instance, is Ike in conversation with Winthrop Aldrich at the London Embassy. Can you get together the two people you mentioned in your message, without embarrassment? asks the President.

   "Aldrich: Yes, one of them I have just been playing bridge with. Perhaps I can stop him.

   President: I'd rather you talk to both together. You know who I mean? One has the same name as my predecessor at Colombia University Presidency (Butler); the other was with me in the war. (Macmillan)

   Aldrich: I know the one with you in the war. Oh yes, now I've got it.

   President: Could you get them informally and say of course we are interested and sympathetic, and as soon as things happen that we anticipate, we can 'furnish a lot of fig leaves'.

   Aldrich: I can certainly say that.

   President: Will that be enough to get the boys going?

   Aldrich: I think it will be."

   This dialogue is recorded on page 460-1 of Carlton's book, and it continues beyond the point here quoted. Aldrich was right. The boys did get moving, and Eden was ditched. Carlton rightly compares their role to that of Janos Kadar in Hungary during the same time. Kadar, of course, in the approved style of the other block, arrived in power after open collisions and brutal shunts. Macmillan, by contrast, enjoyed an elegant apotheosis, more fitting by far. But Carlton is describing the structure of the relationship, not the niceties of its conduct.
4. Philip Williams, Gaitskell's biographer, tells us that after Eden's cumuppance the Suez blunder "was advantageous to its perpetrators . . . and Gaitskell was wise not to keep harping on it". (*Hugh Gaitskell*, Cape, 1979, p. 443) But did Gaitskell then know what Carlton has now told us all?
5. At least 10,000, more likely 15,000 nuclear warheads are emplaced across this divide. The USA has installed between 7,000 and 10,000 of these, the USSR between 3,500 and 5,000. These weapons range from squibs of 30 or 40 kilotons (three Hiroshimas) up to 20 megatons (a Birmingham or two).
6. US military outlays rose 3.7% in 1980 and 5% in 1981. The Soviet Union tries to keep up. World wide weapon expenditure now rises at 3% per annum in volume. No progress at all has been made towards disarmament.
7. Turnstile Press, 1982, p. 161.
8. "The value, or worth of a man, is as of all other things, his price; that is to say, so much as would be given for the use of his power." Leviathan, I, 10.
9. For documentation, see Noam Chomsky and Edward S. Herman, *The Political Economy of Human Rights*, 2 volumes, Spokesman, 1980.

CHAPTER TWELVE

A New Internationalism

In whatever ways the socialist movements of Western Europe think they know better than the Yugoslavs, there is no reasonable dissent from the view that the argument for workers' control and industrial democracy all over our continent has drawn great support from the experience and experiments of the system of self-management. If we consider the ideas of self-management as a model, there is no doubt of its exceptional and specific Yugoslavian nature. Few informed socialists see any possibility of simply transplanting innovations from that country to their own. But if we look instead at the issues and challenges which provoked self-management as a response, and seek out the lessons of this interaction of problem and result, we can all identify rather clear prescriptions within a similar framework. Indeed, such a procedure enables us to learn equally from the failures as well as the successes of Yugoslav practices. Attempts to do this have produced a rich literature, all unforced by state patronage, and each offering witness to a genuine force of example. Certainly the British movement for workers' control owes, and knows that it owes, a considerable debt to this experience.

Surprisingly, the other major contribution of Yugoslavia to the international socialist vocabulary has been little discussed in any of the advanced countries. Yet the concept of non-alignment may soon come to exercise a dominant fascination for West European socialists, to say nothing of their Eastern European equivalents (both "official" and otherwise) during the concluding years of this century.

Obviously, the contemporary question which immediately opens out on to a need for non-aligned policies is that of nuclear disarmament in Europe. We have written about this elsewhere, and this article is not intended to add to the growing debate on the matter. The proposal for a nuclear-free zone, along the lines initiated by the Latin American treaty of Tlatelolco, and endorsed by the United Nations First Special Session on Disarmament in 1978, has aroused very widespread interest and support in Europe. It has been upheld by a conference of the Socialist International, in Madrid in 1980, after assiduous lobbying by the present Prime Minister of Finland, Kalevi Sorsa, and Walter Hacker of the Austrian Socialists. It gave rise to a series of European Conventions which have brought together not only socialists, trade unionists and independent communists, but representatives from all the major peace movements in the West, numerous women's groups, environmentalists, and a cross-section of other political trends from Iceland right down to Italy and Greece. Alva Myrdal, a 1982 Nobel Peace Prize winner, has given us the classic statement of the strategy of this campaign, which implies the ultimate dissolution of the blocs into which Europe has been wrenched since the end of the Second World War. For this most powerful reason the idea of non-alignment has a future in Europe, which otherwise bears the continued risk of a nuclear exchange in the most heavily armed "theatre" of the world, even while it has no direct interests which could by any rational process lead it into this complete madness. The possibility that such a conflict could "spill back" as Myrdal puts it, from war zones in any of the other continents also powerfully underlines the need for a new European policy towards the world of the South, of underdevelopment, poverty and neo-imperial rivalries.

At the level of geo-politics this world has already made its own demands on us. We can read them in the growing pressure for "a new world economic order". The same needs have also been refracted, albeit hazily, through the Brandt Report by a team of concerned (if at the time mostly displaced) Western political leaders.

What the Labour movements of Europe have not yet done is to match this official and semi-official concern with proposals serving their own direct interests, or to explore the possibilities of developing a genuinely alternative economic strategy in which Labour in both North and South begins to challenge capital as the predominant force. The same transnational corporations which overshadow the economies of Europe cast an even greater shade across the Third World. The same international institutions, such as the International Monetary Fund or the World Bank, which use their influence to temper undesirably rash welfare policies in the West are also heavily engaged in restraining over-radical policies by the former colonial territories which have now for two decades been embarking upon Statehood. Investment decisions taken in the name of "development" frequently, if not normally, serve to reinforce dependence. To replace the indigenous East African soap industry with modern detergents does not make Africans any cleaner, but it does substitute the global intervention of the multinationals for local enterprise and raw materials. At the same time, it tilts the balance of payments of the "beneficiary" in an adverse direction.

A similar loss of initiative afflicts British or other European trade unions, still nationally organised and oriented, and imperfectly linked in a Regional Federation which has so far been unable to concert any substantial Governmental policies to restrict the predatory effects of transnational operations. The two major International Federations of trade unions which pretend to organisation on a world scale have had even less practical effect, largely because they have been historically undermined by the political divisions of the cold war. Yet the need for intercontinental contact between employees of the same giant companies is plainly apparent. Long before we can talk of effective international action by trade unions there has to arise a network of practical contacts, at the enterprise level, a persistent exchange of useful bargaining information, and through this a gradual process of convergence on common aims and mutual support.

There is no way that trade unions can avoid facing up to the implications of state policies (and the lack of state policies) in this field. Unions, not less than Governments, are already becoming aware of the general use of transfer prices to frustrate wage claims as well as tax demands. They are often rudely reminded (as again are states) of the capacity that transnationals have to influence behaviour by redirecting investment, or by the actual movement of planned locations. They are often not so aware of the meaning of the transnational influence on trade. A steadily growing proportion of world trade takes place within the transnational corporations themselves. Their influence taken together is absolutely daunting. Michael Barratt Brown has drawn our attention to what must surely be seen as a priority need to develop planned trade as a main lever of development. This is becoming far more crucial than the pursuit of a one-sided call for aid. Trade policies determine what can be made before it can be sold: they can encourage the deployment of actually existing resources as a springboard for the creation of new ones. They can frustrate the imposition of inappropriate choices about products or about the technology to make products. And today who can deny that workers in the collapsing old industries of Britain face this need every bit as urgently as do non-aligned Algerians or Yugoslavs? Aid will not be forthcoming on any scale adequate to regenerate Liverpool or the North-East any more than it has ever lifted vast tracts of Africa or Asia into bare subsistence. There will be no answer to this problem unless steps can be taken towards resolving the prior problem of trade.

One long step towards the de-alignment of Europe is already taking place, with the crystallisation of the International Political and Social Economy project, which launched its programme *Out of Crisis* in March 1983. This ambitious plan was the result of a series of meetings between socialist economists over a period of one decade. Many of these people have since taken up office in different countries, serving as Parliamentarians, members of their Party Executives, or sometimes as Government Ministers. In France, the present Ministers of Finance, and Industry and Commerce, Delors and Chevenement, were among the moving forces of the project, as was Joxe, the Leader of the National Assembly. Premier Papandreou and his economic ministers have also been actively involved from an early stage. Later on, active encouragement came from Bruno Kreisky, as well as Swedish and Spanish Socialist Ministers.

The key animator of this remarkable initiative was Stuart Holland, who brought together economists from the Universities of Cambridge, Paris, Modena, Bremen and Madrid to elaborate a detailed programme for concerned reflation coupled with integrated restructuring and redistribution of resources. This plan calls for "better-my-neighbour" policies of reflation which would, if pursued with adequate support, help create several million new jobs within a decade. The supporting context involves major redistribution between firms and sectors of the economy; between social classes; and between more and less developed regions. The project is European in a continental sense, not at all restricted to the countries of the EEC. It offers an alternative perspective which could, if thoroughly pursued, displace the dominance of the IMF itself, and begin a turn towards new patterns of international economic co-operation. Whilst holding to radical objectives, it admits of encroaching implementation, and does not depend upon simultaneous adhesion by all European Governments. Indeed, it plans for a rolling programme of supporting actions, which assumes a cumulative effect as one Government after another is brought into participation. Stuart Holland himself sees it as a contribution to answering the "three Ms", multinationals, militarism and monetarism, with an alternative to crisis and crisis-deepening political management.

The IPSE forum will continue its work in a series of meetings which have already been scheduled, and it is important that trade unionists should relate to these by advancing their own constructive proposals, and offering their own experiences. Some of these turn on the issue of planning agreements, and others open what is at this moment a new territory.

In Britain, the movement for workers' control has been gravely hampered by the fact that four million people have been displaced from work. This has eroded trade union influence, stalemated some important workshop powers, and begun to range some unions against others in a sad game of divide and rule. Membership loss in some unions has been grave. In general, trade union militancy has been restricted to two categories of employment: economically sheltered or untypically prosperous firms, usually in the transnational sector; and the growing slum sectors of the public services, where wages have been forced down to subsistence levels and resistance has been seen as a last, often desperate resort.

The result of all this has been to move experiments in industrial democracy into the field of worker co-operatives, and into the area of local authority enterprise. A lively school of municipal socialism has thus emerged. Under the influence of workers' corporate plans such as that of the Lucas Combine Shop Stewards' Committee, local Councillors have sought to find how to match needs to resources, creating new industrial opportunities in the ruins of moneterrorism.

But any enterprise must distribute its product, whether in the social market of the welfare sector, or in the market place. Most new workers' co-operatives will be unable to avoid this market place, and a socialist trade policy will remain quite crucial for them. For this reason, they should address themselves to the IPSE forum, and also seek to form direct links with co-operatives and municipalities elsewhere, not only in Europe, but further afield.

The mechanisms for doing this could be greatly improved by

governmental and municipal co-ordination. There is a strong case for a meeting of socialist municipalities in Europe, aimed at better interaction in this sector, and at a collective effort to help open co-operative trading relations with the Third World.

Some of this could happen quickly. Some of it is already happening. All of it will be easier when socialists begin to see their responsibilities outside the old framework which is now a scaffold of crisis and polarisation. It is time to begin moving towards a new world of non-aligned co-operation.

CHAPTER THIRTEEN

An Interview*

Thesis Eleven: Social democracy is a term that can be used to describe both a type of political party and a type of social order. Concentrating, for the moment, on the first usage, we should note that it was initially applied to those parties, especially in central Europe, that were affiliated to the Second (Socialist) International. There is, of course, a (discontinuous) line of descent between these parties, and contemporary political parties such as the German SPD and the Australian and British Labour Parties, which are affiliated to the modern Socialist International. But some (Salvadori, for example) would argue that, in terms of political ideology, the modern Eurocommunist parties are the real heirs to the traditions of the Second International. How would you view the relationship between the Second International tradition and the modern social democratic and Eurocommunist parties?

Ken Coates: We are in danger when we approach evolving political organisms only through our perception of their "traditions". There are abrupt discontinuities in socialist history. Some were generalised, as was that disastrous cleavage which annulled autonomous socialist politics in Europe for two decades and more after the Second World War. This locked "national" communisms into Stalinism and most social-democratic parties into the Atlantic bloc. As Braunthal points out in his *History*, it would have been inconceivable for socialist parties to acknowledge the leadership of the capitalist United States, before the traumas of the late 'forties.

Other socialist parties have been reduced to almost nothing (notably that in France, after the disasters of the war with Egypt and the Algerian conflict) and then reconstituted on a quite different basis. Some have been reborn after long repression under

*This interview was given to the Australian journal *Thesis Eleven*.

dictatorships (Spain, Portugal, Greece). The British Labour Party has undergone important sociological changes as well as political convulsions.

The ideological traditions of both Second and Third Internationals have been fairly criticised by a variety of alternative marxisms and new left activisms, and all this activity has been reflected within the given party structures.

What remains paramount in Europe is the need for a convergence of the left on autonomous politics, free of Soviet and US patronage, aimed at co-ordinating economic policy to restore employment, and also aimed at developing new international relations which can both break the arms race and turn to the establishment of a new trade pattern to assist third world development.

Thesis Eleven: In speaking of social democratic parties, we have assumed that the parties affiliated to the Socialist International are essentially homogeneous in ideology, structure etc. Yet some would point to certain very obvious lines of division. One such line is that between those continental European socialist and social democratic parties, which drew their strength originally from a mass individual membership, mobilised around a socialist political ideology, and those "Anglo-Saxon" labour parties, which were based initially on the trade union movement, and which aspired to represent the labour movement as a whole, rather than its specifically socialist elements. How important has this distinction been historically, and how important is it today? Do you believe it is possible for a labour party ever to become an effective socialist party?

Ken Coates: The virtue of federalism on the British and Australian patterns is that it is normally responsive to democratic pressures. Anyone who helps renew the drive to democratisation of modern institutions is reopening all that is nowadays relevant in the socialist project. Whether this will succeed is an open question, but it *could* succeed. All other proposals would fail even if they did "succeed".

Thesis Eleven: Both parliamentarians and trade union officials play an important, perhaps dominant, role in the internal politics of social democratic and labour parties (although, historically, the role of trade union officials has probably been of even greater significance in the case of the latter than in that of the former). It could be argued that the structural position of parliamentarians, as politicians concerned to win votes, and of trade union officials, as arbitrators between capital and labour, concerned to resolve industrial disputes, predisposes each towards a certain political conservatism. Do you believe this to be the case? And, if so, does this represent an insuperable obstacle to the radicalisation of such parties? Is there, as Michels argued, an 'iron law of oligarchy' at work within both parties and unions? If not, how might a radicalisation of both parties and unions be achieved?

Ken Coates: It is high time to debunk Michels. He wrote when English children left school at twelve, often without rudimentary literacy. His oligarchs ran schools in "oratory". Today's European working class doesn't listen to "oratory". It is vastly better schooled, technically better qualified, better informed even by a manipulated mass communications system, and habituated to three decades of relatively full employment. We can also counter oligarchy by a wide range of democratic pressures which are widely understood. The "conservatism" of modern oligarchs exists, but it, like their powers, rests on a consent which arises from the failure of cogent alternative proposals. This failure can be rectified, and then we shall see how "iron" the law of oligarchy actually is.

Thesis Eleven: Social democratic, labour, and Eurocommunist parties share a common commitment to reform, as a means either to the amelioration of capitalism or to the gradual attainment of socialism. But there is an alternative political tradition, represented not only by Leninism, by also by anarchism, syndicalism (the I.W.W., for example), and by theorists such as Luxemburg, Trotsky and, arguably, Gramsci, that stresses the need for an eventual revolutionary overthrow of the capitalist state. Clearly, neither the reformist nor the revolutionary tradition has proven especially successful in achieving a 'socialist transformation' in the advanced capitalist countries. How would you evaluate the respective claims of both reformist and revolutionary socialism? Leaving aside the possible limitations of revolutionary socialism, what, if any, are the limitations of reform?

Ken Coates: Reform was contained within a framework of Keynesian remedies whilst the postwar international economic order remained intact, simply because this framework appeared to "work". When the Keynesian world order collapsed this reflected the fact that multinational capital had evaded more and more of the controls imposed by individual nation states, so that such states could no longer effectively manage their "own" economies. Now those remedies cannot be simply scaled down to the national scale, so that "reform" is only possible on an international scale. "Revolution" on that scale is even more difficult, because nuclear weapons must make all rational people cautious about how they disturb the balances.

The limitations of Reform are primarily based upon the fact that reforming institutions have here been tempted to initiate action at inappropriate levels. Europe could reflate and create jobs where France or Greece cannot. Autarchy and fortress solutions always cost more in democratic choice than people are willing to pay, although they will become unavoidable if we do not break through to convergent international action on a sustainable programme.

Thesis Eleven: Dispite the many differences between the Stalinist Communist tradition and that of the social democratic and labour parties, they each share a common commitment to the political goal of 'state socialism' (governed either by the totalitarian or by the parliamentary state), and to the political strategy of 'socialism from above' (directed either by the professional-military or by the parliamentary party). Yet there are alternative currents, within both Marxist and non-Marxist socialism, that would aspire to a much more libertarian vision of socialism (based, for example, on workers' councils or on some form of 'self-management'), and that would stress the importance of 'self-activity' and 'self-emancipation' in attaining such a goal. Such ideas have, of course, exercised a profound influence on the evolution of the many and varied currents of 'New Left' opinion that have appeared since 1956. Do the current social democratic versions of 'state socialism' and 'socialism from above' represent an adequate response to the political dilemmas of late capitalism? If not, how might they be modified so as to incorporate elements of this alternative, libertarian politics? Or is such an incorporation effectively impossible?

Ken Coates: What can be done with modern information technology can lead to greater centralism and greater democracy at the same time. Autonomy was always a very partial answer to bureaucratic centralism, because it is either rested on market relations which themselves promoted injustice, or upon lesser autocracies rather than greater ones. Socialism still needs its counter to market forces. But it also needs free institutions, a relevant separation of powers, and a democratic political theory and practice which has still not emerged, either in the traditional parties or the New Left.

Thesis Eleven: To be more specific, how important do you believe the policy objective of nationalisation to be to the socialist project? And, in so far as it is important, what forms should such nationalisations take?

Ken Coates: If planning and co-ordination result from democratic argument, then nationalisation need not differ substantially from co-operative enterprise. Without socialisation of the entrepreneurial function, we have no hope of regenerating our societies, which will then remain divided into three classes: unemployed helots and transnational company employees at the level of subjection, with militaristic autocrats ruling over them. I doubt whether civilisation will enter the next millenium if this process is not halted. Therefore we need a laboratory of democratic industrial initiatives. In Britain, this has struggled to establish itself in such experiments as the Lucas Aerospace Shop Stewards' Corporate Plan, and numerous Local Government Planning agencies.

Thesis Eleven: In most advanced capitalist countries (the obvious exception being the United States), social democratic, labour and, occasionally, Eurocommunist parties represent the major institutional foci for organised, radical politics. But many radicals prefer to work outside such parties, either as activists within 'single issue' political movements or within trade unions, or as members of smaller left parties and sects. Do you believe that socialists should be actively engaged in the internal politics of social democratic and labour parties? If so, what should be their goals (should they, for example, aim to shift those parties in a socialist direction, or should they aim to build a socialist current within those parties that might provide the political basis for an eventually separate socialist party)? If not, what should be their goals, and how should they relate to the existing social democratic and labour parties?

Ken Coates: I can see no point in remaining outside the political process if you have any possibility of influencing it in the direction you wish it to take. I am impatient with socialists who tell us that their purity will suffer in any practical engagement. They are like the legendary Irishman, who, when asked the way to Cork, replied

"Cork? If I was going there I wouldn't start from here!" Certainly we have all learnt from some philosophers who were not very practical people. But few of us are so in touch with the infinite that our undefilement with reality can help us. Most of us learn more from trying than we do from discouraging effort.

Thesis Eleven: To be more specific, what have been, and what should be, the relationships, between the mass working class political parties, on the one hand, and the various 'mass movements' (for example, the anti-nuclear and ecology movements), on the other? Do such movements constitute, as some would claim, an alternative politics to those of the mass parties of the left?

Ken Coates: No, issue-centred lobbies are not an alternative to politics. Sometimes they become political parties, but then they have to engage all the problems they previously rejected. In politics we have to find related answers to give us work, peace, and freedom. We shall not find these goods locked in boxes at the ends of separate roads.

Thesis Eleven: Since the mid 1970s, the world capitalist system has experienced a serious economic crisis. On one account, one might expect such a crisis to lead to mass disillusion with capitalism, and hence to an increased electoral support for social democratic and labour parties, and to a shift to the left in the politics of these parties. The former has clearly occurred in France, and the latter, to some extent, in Britain. But, in general, there appears to be little movement in either direction. An alternative account might suggest that reform programmes become less credible in times of crisis (simply because the system has less to offer, by way of concessions to subordinate groups, in times of straightened economic circumstances). What are the political prospects for contemporary social democracy? And how practicable do you expect social democratic reform programmes to prove in the immediate future?

Ken Coates: I have answered this question already. Millions will support reform if they can see how to achieve it. Nation states do not permit it in isolation from one another. Even revolutionary nation states find their options painfully restricted. The main avenue to reform today lies through co-ordinated international action for peace, jobs and democracy. Democracy as *self*-determination depends more and more on mutual *inter*-national support. If socialists, communists, greens and anti-nuclear campaigners can reach agreement to set out together along this way, they might accomplish something. If they cannot, they will suffer crisis, dictatorship and war. Their only comfort will be that it will probably be over quickly.

Thesis Eleven: By comparison with both the pre-1914 socialist parties and the early Communist parties (and perhaps, even, the not-so-early Communist parties), one obvious feature of contemporary social democracy is its lack of intellectual vigour. Social democratic and labour parties normally possess neither theorists of the intellectual calibre of Luxemburg or Kautsky, nor even often the institutional framework within which such theorists might prosper (theoretical journals, party schools, party presses, etc.). Why is this so? How might such a state of affairs be remedied (or is it a matter of no consequence)? In what ways do you believe socialist intellectuals should attempt, not merely to interpret, but also to change the world?

Ken Coates: I do not think the left is an intellectual desert. I know of no period in history when there were more books on socialism. If I were asked who can be most helpful among theorists with a practical slant, I would commend Stuart Holland and Michael Barratt Brown among writers on the economy, and Alva Myrdal on peace and disarmament. But the debate is vitally alive, and there are hundreds of valid contributions.

Thesis Eleven: In the years since the Second World War, social democractic and labour parties have generally become increasingly preoccupied with electoral politics. Some would argue that contemporary social democracy can be defined, not in terms of its role in the electoral process as a party of alternative government, but as concerned essentially to secure office merely for its own sake. To what extent do you believe this to be true? In so far as it is true, what relevance do social democratic and labour parties have to the socialist project today?

Ken Coates: Socialists who cannot win elections cannot make revolutions. Socialists who can do the one might not need to do the other, unless we are talking tautologically. Peace, jobs and democracy world-wide would be, would it not, a revolution?